Praise for *The Most Successful Small Business in the World*

"Michael has laid out the steps that any entrepreneur should take if they truly want to become successful. Get ready to welcome a new wave of successful small businesses into society!"

—Bill Bartmann
Best-selling author of *Bailout Riches*
and a leading authority on entrepreneurship in America

"While Michael's new book is aimed at the fundamental principles needed to build the 'best small businesses,' his material also addresses the leadership gap in our society. Michael points out that our leadership failures are a result of losing touch with our inner self, which results in a lack of higher purpose in life. Our lack of self-awareness is due to too many external distractions. Thus, we have drowned in the river of 'reaction,' which has brought about the massive failure of our institutions. His ten principles are wonderful medicine for our time, bringing us back to the reality that inner perfection leads to outer achievement, integrity attracts profit, and substance defines beautiful form. This book is about awakening to the gift with which we are all born, as well as how to polish that gift with tender and practical care. It is a gem—simple, direct, practical, and beautiful. I love it!"

—Raymond T. Yeh
Co-author, *The Art of Business*

"What could be more important to our economy and future success than learning the secrets of how to build *The Most Successful Small Business in the World* from the guru who changed the world through his best selling E-Myth books? This book is an entrepreneur's dream come true."

—Jason Dietch
Co-Author of National Best Seller, *Discover Wellness—
How Staying Healthy Can Make You Rich*

"Michael's understanding of entrepreneurship and small business management has been a difference maker for countless businesses, including Infusion Software."

—Clate Mask
CEO and Founder, Infusionsoft

"I love my new business, I am jazzed. My team is jazzed. Our clients love it. My life is profoundly affected. I did not realize business could be so much fun. We change lives every day. What a gift. Thank you Michael for your love and passion. What an honor to be coached by you."

—Arif Balagam
Lumina Dental Spa

"Michael Gerber puts the passion back in business! He'll remind you what got you started in the first place, and show you how to get back on track. Instead of uncertainty and frustration, let Michael Gerber give you clarity and wisdom!"

—**Peter Leeds**
CEO of PennyStocks.com

"Michael Gerber's Dreaming Room and his vision of the transformation of mankind through entrepreneurship has inspired us to live our business with passion—Divine Passion!"

—**Bill Dedek**
Sirrus Consulting

"Michael Gerber's ability to get to the core of an issue in the shortest period of time is simply astounding. We attended a Dreaming Room and came out with a fresh perspective and goal which resulted in our completing the manuscript for a book. He encouraged us to share our story. We did, and the process continues to open new doors for us on a constant basis. Thank you, Michael."

—**Bill and Colleen Hensley**
Authors of the upcoming book, *The Pilot—Learning Leadership*

"Going to Micheal Gerber's 'In The Dreaming Room' was one of the best investments into my life and my business. Michael was able to hone onto what my passions were. Most especially he had me realize my 'Big Why' for creating a company where entrepreneurs are holding each other accountable to their dreams through powerful relationships. Since the event, Peer Success Circles has grown internationally and we are now licensing components to other organizations. A big Amen to E-Myth legend Michael Gerber."

—**Joseph Varghese**
Peer Success Circles, joseph@SuccessCircles.com

"Michael is my only *business-roshi*. He is a true master of life first, and of the game of business, second. Even more impressive than his beautifully-crafted stories, is the presence of this man in real life. When you come in contact with him, you can't help but to experience the wisdom and positive energy he radiates. Michael lives his life the way he teaches. Every day, adding a new musical note to the rich and magnificent symphony of his life's work"

—**Cenmar A. Fuertes**
Founder and CEO, CoachLink and Sparkle Restoration Services, Inc.

"Michael Gerber is a world-class unstoppable entrepreneurial guru . . . the greatest business visionary of our time. He is precious and very rare with enormous insight as well as humour. Michael has taught me how to turn my dreams into a business world without boundaries. His words must be cherished and his life lessons learned."

—**Chris Owen**
Marketing Director, LEEDS

"A year of mentoring with Michael Gerber is akin to a lifetime at business school. Our business development journey together has been magnificent. I always feel supported and supercharged by Michael's genius, passion, and energy."

—Peter Wallman
Founder and CEO of Passion Maps,
and Author of *The Wisdom of Passion*

"I am no longer afraid to dream. I am no longer afraid to act. Michael Gerber gave me the courage to build the enterprise that was in me."

—Dave McGrath
Gold Coast Australia

"Meeting and becoming familiar with Michael Gerber and the gift he shares has been an eye opener for me. This experience has caused me to rethink, perhaps several times, the ways I have previously engaged as an entrepreneur. Now, clearly, I can move forward confidently with any new idea in business."

—Dr. Fred Eckfeld

"Michael is an unparalleled exemplar of hope. His words have a magical way of empowering you to challenge and create the impossible—and creating the impossible is the current benchmark of business today!"

—Dusty Emerson
President of Kromatik

"Michael Gerber has once again had a powerful affect on me and is changing the way I start and run my businesses. Michael's insights and instructions for creating and running a successful business will pay huge dividends in all areas of my business and personal life."

—Eric Zapf
Founder of Wet Kiss Creative, Co-inventor of SLAPITZ™,
and Creator of Boulder Bar Endurance

"His insights into how to run a business and make it truly work have provided clarity to me that has helped me see new direction and potential in my business. No one should start or run a business without being a student of Michael's work!"

—Garry Mumford
Insight Associates

"The true entrepreneur is the crystal ball, dreaming the future of the world into its very existence."

—Hugh Morris
President, GRO-PEC Solutions LLC

"With Michael E. Gerber's systematic, holistic approach for building the framework of a business, my whole world has been revolutionized."

—Magnus Still
Chairman, StillArt Enterprises

"Michael Gerber challenged me to 'find an unsolved problem, then make a transformational impact by solving it.' Thanks to his guidance, I set aside self-centered ideals and created an effective and unique solution to a very real need in our society."

—Marnee Weber
The Caregiving Coach

"Michael proved to me hands down that a spiritually based company and smart business savvy can—and should—coexist perfectly! I am forever grateful for Michael's sincere attention and inspiration."

—Rev. Nina Roe
Founder AngelsTeach.com

"Michael's techniques and philosophies go beyond standard business books. His passion and motivation is infectious and demonstrates business is about stepping up to the mark and making a difference, not just to the business owner's life but to others as well."

—Paul Gordon
Managing Director Fit4all Ltd.

"The Man, Michael E. Gerber, is a voice that was sent into the world to ignite the true entrepreneur to focus and succeed. Every successful person that I have met has made comments on how Michael Gerber's E-Myth books have changed their lives. Where would millions of Entrepreneur's lives and business be without the Man of Michael E. Gerber?"

—Phenon Walker
Cleveland, Ohio

"The brilliance of a man can be seen through his work. Reading his books and working with him for over a year now there is no doubt in my mind that the brilliance of Michael E. Gerber shines through everything he does. A true master of his craft."

—Randy Ansems
Canadian Entrepreneur

"I rediscovered the passion that had been lost when I finished my professional baseball career. By regaining the sense of joy and satisfaction that comes from rediscovering your life's Assignment—rediscovering that it's all about *Who You Are* in creating value in the lives of people God brings across your path. Thanks, Michael, for unlocking the 30-year void in my heart and turning me into the leader in business that I remember being in sports!"

—**Randy Hammon**
Founder, My Retirement Coach, Inc.

"*Work on it, not in it.* That changed absolutely everything . . . "

—**Scott Hedrick**
Founder, JustBats.com

"Michael's tools and books have inspired me to dream big and put into reality my vision to help turn around business failure in the United States and help entrepreneurs get off to a fast start to profits! He has the rare ability not only to reach down into your core and bring out your best but also to propel you to massive action!"

—**Scott Letourneau**
www.FastBusinessStartUp.com and www.FastBusinessCredit.com

"I had the good fortune of attending a Dreaming Room event with Michael last year and it was an experience I will never forget. You cannot be a successful entrepreneur without reading Michael's books, and experiencing him live In the Dreaming Room is nothing short of life-changing."

—**Stephanie Chandler**
Author, speaker, consultant; www.StephanieChandler.com

"Michael and The Dreaming Room have dramatically expanded my belief in both what I am capable of and how big my company can grow."

—**Steve Kelsey**
Printhink Solutions Inc.

"Michael Gerber didn't just break my thinking out-of-the-box, he helped me see how I could build my business in its own special shape. Everything looked different after that!"

—**Susan Schwartz**
You Who Branding

"Michael Gerber encouraged me to dream bigger than I ever imagined possible. What I had believed impossible became possible by learning how to sort out my dream, vision, mission and purpose in a systematic way. He will impact you for the rest of your life, like he did to me."

—KC Kang
President, Authentic Ways, Inc.;
Author of *More than Skin Deep, 3 Secrets to finding Authentic Beauty*

"The process turns you inside out and shakes you upside down to see what has been hiding deep inside. Scary—yes! Exciting—absolutely! The most exciting is not only what it will do to help you but in how you will help to improve the world."

—Dr. Wanda Lee MacPhee
www.stmargaretsbaychiro.com

"(He) gave me permission to Dream Big and taught me to start small. He let me listen to my inner voice. I'm now ready and well on my way to make my dream come true."

—Deborah S. Sarnoff, MD

"Michael has been the 'Rosetta Stone' in helping me distinguish my day dreams to the DREAM that is my higher self's purpose and mission for my life. His dreaming room is a SPACE that is safe, YET engaging, empowering, surprising, rewarding, and challenged a breakthrough to what mattered to me."

—Mark Rolando Rosales
www.cardiograde.com

"My Dreaming Room experiences along with Michael's mentorship have had a dramatic impact on my business insight. With Michael's unmatched enthusiasm and point-on advice, my dreams of owning a world class business will soon be my reality!"

—Thomas Drexler

THE MOST SUCCESSFUL SMALL BUSINESS IN THE WORLD

THE MOST SUCCESSFUL SMALL BUSINESS IN THE WORLD

THE TEN PRINCIPLES®

MICHAEL E. GERBER

WILEY

John Wiley & Sons, Inc.

Published by John Wiley & Sons, Inc., Hoboken, New Jersey.
Published simultaneously in Canada.

For general information on our other products and services or for technical support, please contact our Customer Care Department within the United States at (800) 762-2974, outside the United States at (317) 572-3993 or fax (317) 572-4002.

Wiley also publishes its books in a variety of electronic formats. Some content that appears in print may not be available in electronic books. For more information about Wiley products, visit our web site at www.wiley.com.

Library of Congress Cataloging-in-Publication Data:

Gerber, Michael E.
   The most successful small business in the world : the ten principles® / by Michael E. Gerber.
        p. cm.
   Includes bibliographical references and index.
   ISBN 978-0-470-50362-1 (cloth : acid-free paper)
   1. Small business.   I. Title.
   HD2341.G47 2010
   658.02'2–dc22

                                                           2009038789

Printed in the United States of America

10 9 8 7 6 5 4 3 2 1

He who has a why to live for can bear
with almost any how . . .
—Nietzsche

Contents

Foreword

My first encounter with Michael Gerber was Divine Providence. It was certainly more than coincidence (and in any case, I share Einstein's view that "coincidence is G-d's way of remaining anonymous").

When I first met Mr. Gerber, I was 36 years old, and he was 71. I had been working as a Chabad rabbi in Malibu, California, for 13 years. Like all Chabad emissaries, I was moved and inspired by our great leader, Rabbi Menachem M. Schneerson, best known simply as "The Rebbe."

The Rebbe arrived in America after fleeing Nazi-occupied Europe. In response to the atrocities of the war, he determined that the world needed a profound and lasting reorientation and set out to make it happen. He believed that if one evil human being could bring such tragedy to our planet, then certainly a concentrated effort, involving millions of people, could create a world of goodness and kindness.

The Rebbe envisioned our world as G-d intended it to be—one where the beautiful, Divine potential that exists in all of us is present in every aspect of our lives. He stated that selfishness, anger, and jealousy are all products of a "cover-up"—and when the mask is lifted, our inner beings can shine through. The result will be a world of true inner peace, joy, and harmony.

When I read Michael Gerber's book *The E-Myth Revisited*, I had a surprising spiritual experience that made me feel that I must meet the writer. I was touched by his words: "I will never again let the curtain go down." Something about that sentiment and the work that I do as a Chabad rabbi told me that Mr. Gerber's methods and attitude could help me achieve my work on behalf of the Rebbe's dream.

I was aware that Michael Gerber had been an inspiration to thousands of small business owners and that he might not be easy to reach, but that never stopped me. Despite my calling the wrong office to contact him, somehow he received the message that a rabbi was trying to reach him. We made an appointment, and together with a few other rabbis we had our first meeting.

I will forever cherish the energy of that encounter. In my line of work, I constantly meet with people of all ages and backgrounds. I find that when people reach a certain stage in life, they're often content with who they are and what they do—or at least, they accept their current place in the world. While this sense of satisfaction may have some benefits, the Rebbe spoke strongly about never being content when it comes to our spiritual growth.

Michael Gerber exuded a gentle, yet strong spirit that was inspiring. Here was a man in his seventies who could easily retire—yet the youthful, ever-seeking energy within him wouldn't consider anything of the sort. He had a vital exuberance as if he'd just gotten started with his entrepreneurial passion. He was like a 25-year-old trapped in a 71-year-old body. It was extraordinary.

I remember Michael telling us about his limited involvement with Judaism—including the rabbi who convinced him not to become one—as well as the other great "inspirational moments" connected to his Jewish upbringing. But there was one story that validated my desire to meet him.

Michael described the time when he joined a group who wanted to get together so they could discuss Jewish culture. In one of the first meetings, Michael brought up the "scary"

elephant in the room that everyone else seemed to be avoiding—
he expressed the fact that if they were going to do something
Jewish together, then surely G-d must be part of the discussion.
When his suggestion was denied, he decided to opt out.

Why did this intrigue me so much? It intrigued me because
our world has become accustomed to avoiding the important
questions. We have stopped seeking. We have stopped talking to
our inner child.

We routinely dodge the core philosophical questions, such as
what is the purpose of life? Why does one get married? Why does
one have children? What do we really want out of life? Fundamental issues have become unwelcome topics in our day-to-day
lives as we are caught up in the material world around us, as we
try to earn a living and provide for our families.

And here was a man who still wanted to explore. Here was a
man who was unwilling to make any issue—even the "G-d"
issue—off limits. A true breath of fresh air.

Being alive requires a constant expression of life. Things that
have life grow. People grow, animals grow, plants grow—only
lifeless stones cannot grow.

Michael Gerber is committed to growth, and his gift is to help
others grow as well. He hit the mark when he wrote, "[M]ost
business owners are not entrepreneurs, but technicians suffering
from an entrepreneurial seizure." He himself is not just a technician. He hasn't closed the door on his inner child by silencing
questions, and just going through the motions. He is living his
mantra in his own ongoing journey of personal discovery.

I now realize that when Michael is communicating his
message to business owners, he is actually sharing his deep desire
that others remain open and connected to their inner child.

Wikipedia defines an entrepreneur as "a person who has
possession of an enterprise, or venture, and assumes significant

accountability for the inherent risks and the outcome." He or she is someone who is willing to converse with their inner child, despite the risks and fears involved with what and where it may bring them.

As Michael puts it, "a business without a dream is like a life without a purpose"—and an entrepreneur is always connected to the dream, because he is also thinking about his purpose.

I can tell you that Michael Gerber is just the man I was looking for when I tracked down the inspiring author of *The E-Myth Revisited*. His partnership and participation in the Rebbe's dream continues to be invaluable.

In these pages, I expect that you will discover a soulful approach toward your future goals, and I pray that you too, will never close the door on your inner child.

—Rabbi Levi Cunin
Malibu, California

"The annals of American business are filled with 'impossible dreams' that have come true. I believe in those dreams, and most importantly, I believed in my dream."

—Mary Kay Ash
The Mary Kay Way

A Brief Introduction

"But I am being reborn and I need to take new risks."
—Paulo Coelho
The Zahir

I have been thinking about this book and writing it in my mind's eye since my very first book, *The E-Myth: Why Most Small Businesses Don't Work and What to Do About It*, was published in 1986.

Since then, an intense, but not nearly active enough, dialogue has ensued between me and my readers throughout the world.

Intense, because to a person who owns a broken small business (as most of my readers do), the thesis that I raised in *The E-Myth* has found a treasured place in their hearts and minds (more about that in a moment).

Not nearly active enough, because although I have spoken with thousands of readers over the past three decades, I have not had a personal dialogue with most of the more than three million business owners and entrepreneurs who have read some or all of my books.

- Readers—like you, perhaps—who have read *The E-Myth* but have never contacted me to discuss what I shared with you in the book and what happened to you after you read it.

- Readers like many others who never even thought to contact me because the reader of a book doesn't think that the author would be interested in having a conversation with them, or would ever respond to them if they did.

- Readers like still others who once having read the book, or a part of it (yes, there are many I know who start a book and never finish it) go back to their business without ever having thought that in writing the book I was actually speaking to them, not just to some mythical small business stranger next door.

- Readers who didn't realize that *The E-Myth* thesis directly applied to them.

- Readers who didn't know that they were, indeed, the Sarah with whom I carried on a conversation in many of my books. Sarah was the owner of a pie shop that was eating her alive.

I wish I could know who those millions of readers are. For that matter, I wish I could know who *you* are as you read this book. I wish I could know what's going on in your mind, in your life, in your business. I wish we could have a conversation, you and I . . .

So that the meaning of the book you hold in your hands could become immediately transparent to you.

So that you could put it to use.

So that you could use it to create your own personal revolution, as I have created mine.

I wish that because you are the reason that I write the books I write. I write my books for you.

For all entrepreneurs.

For all small business owners.

For all those who dream.

Not for some theoretical you. But, for the very same you who is reading this book and who will, following the last page of this book, put the book down and do with it what you will.

I write my books for the many, many millions of others just like you whose lives could be significantly greater, if only they would take my message to heart by following the regimen recounted within.

In short, I write to provide you with my experience.

I write to provide you with the sum total of what I have learned from the tens of thousands of small business owners, just like you, with whom I've worked throughout the world.

I write to save you from the countless wasted hours you would spend, the frustrations you would experience, the unnecessary pain resulting from trying to build a small business (as most small business owners do), for all the wrong reasons. And, as a result of those missteps, you would produce nowhere near the results you could produce . . . should produce . . . if only you will follow the right-way path I have laid out for you in this book.

But, let me tell you from an author's perspective—mine at least (I don't know what other authors think about or care about)—that your life, your business, your thoughts, your concerns, your frustrations, and your successes, have everything to do with what I write about, think about, and do each and every day of my life.

Let me say it again. I write about you, and for you, and for the stunning accomplishments that are waiting for you, if only you will see them. If only you awaken to them. If only you come to the understanding that, while these accomplishments I write about might seem too grand, too expansive, they are all within your reach.

That brings us to this book, the book you are holding in your hands right now. This book is quite special to me. And, if I am right, equally special for you.

It's called *The Most Successful Small Business in the World*, because in long or in short, that is the theme of every book I've written, although I have never before quite stated it like that. I have never told you before that the business you are thinking of creating, or the business that you own today, could actually become the Most Successful Small Business in the World.

But, it can. And that's the point.

In this book I intend to teach you exactly how to conceive and then build the Most Successful Small Business in the World. Because nothing less will do.

THE TEN PRINCIPLES

According to the *New Oxford American Dictionary*, a principle is "[a] fundamental truth or proposition that serves as the foundation for a system of belief or behavior or for a chain of reasoning."

In my mind, there are 10 such principles that underlie the creation of the Most Successful Small Business in the World:

The First Principle: A small business, built rightly can grow 10,000 times its current size.

The Second Principle: A small business is no more effective than the idea upon which it is built.

The Third Principle: A small business is a system in which all parts contribute to the success or failure of the whole.

The Fourth Principle: A small business must be sustainable through all economic conditions, in all markets, providing meaningful, highly differentiated results to all of its customers.

The Fifth Principle: A small business is a school in which its employees are students, with the intention, will, and determination to grow.

The Sixth Principle: A small business must manifest the higher purpose upon which it was seeded, the vision it was meant to exemplify, the mission it was intended to fulfill.

The Seventh Principle: A small business is the fruit of a higher aim in the mind of the person who conceived it.

The Eighth Principle: A small business possesses a life of its own, in the service of G-d, in whom it finds reason.

The Ninth Principle: A small business is an economic entity, driving an economic reality, creating an economic certainty for the communities in which it thrives.

The Tenth Principle: A small business creates a standard against which all small businesses are measured as either successful, or not, to upgrade the possibility for all small businesses to thrive beyond the standards that formerly existed, whether stated or not.

THE E-MYTH THESIS

So, there you have it: The Ten Principles upon which to conceive, grow, and expand your company.

That is the content of this book. It's a small book, but an essential book. An essential book, because it provides, for the first time, an understanding of the standards upon which your thinking must be measured for you to make a significant difference in the world, while realizing your entrepreneurial objectives.

In each chapter, I devote myself to explaining one of the Ten Principles to make them cogent, understandable, actionable, and translatable into a company that you can verify is the Most Successful Small Business in the World.

How will you know? Because it exemplifies the Ten Principles to a tee. Because the Ten Principles will live at the heart of your business for everyone to see. Because the Ten Principles will speak loudly and clearly to everyone who works in your company, buys from your company, invests in your company, and thrives in the communities your company serves.

That brings us then to the E-Myth thesis that I spoke about earlier. What the E-Myth says is really quite simple:

It says that most business owners are not entrepreneurs, but technicians suffering from an entrepreneurial seizure.

It says that entrepreneurs go to work *on* their business, not just *in* their business, to build a perfect operating system that becomes the brand of their business.

It says that great companies are built by great imaginations, and that great imaginations live in all of us if we allow them to—if we sustain them, nurture them, treasure them, and regard them as our highest gift from G-d.

It says that the system is the solution; if your business does not possess a highly differentiated way of doing business, your company can never excel as the Most Successful Small Business in the World, or come even close to it.

It says that you are the source of the great idea of your business, and the great idea of your business is the source of success experienced by your business.

It says that you too can do this thing that I am writing about in this book, to the degree you are moved by it.

And it says if you are not moved by it, your business will suffer, your people will suffer, and your life will suffer. They will suffer because you didn't reach high enough. You didn't reach high enough, not because you didn't know how to—I can teach that to you!—but because you didn't care to or didn't dare to.

Let that form the foundation for the reading you are about to do.

If you care to, you will dare to.
And nothing else will be required of you,
other than the will.

—Michael E. Gerber
Carlsbad, California

" . . . then I was a young man a thousand years old, and now I am an old man waiting to be born."

—Charles Bukowski
Sifting Through the Madness for the Word, the Line, the Way

Chapter 1

The First Principle

A Small Business, Built Rightly, Can Grow 10,000 Times Its Current Size

The loftier the building, the deeper the foundation must be laid.

—Thomas Kempis

Had each and every one of my previous books begun with this First Principle, we would probably be having a completely different conversation right now. Either more people would have read my books, or fewer would have.

This is because only an infinitesimal number of new business owners start their new business with a notion of size other than the word "small." And that's why their businesses never grow beyond their notion.

Most businesses, no matter their age, remain *adamantly* small.

Note that 70 percent of all companies and 100 percent of home businesses are sole proprietorships. One person, or two, and that's all, operate the business. These businesses are populated by owners working for a living. They are working at a job and nothing more. But of course that's all they ever wanted to do. All they ever wanted to do was to create a job; to create control over their personal income; to create a place to work, a place to do what they know how to do. Or, if not that, to do something, anything, through which they can turn their labor and ideas into money. In short, they want to be self-employed.

Needless to say, these commercial activities are not businesses at all; not in the context we speak of here. They are gardeners gardening. They are architects bending over their boards. They are therapists tending to their flocks. They are rabbis teaching. They are doers doing what doers do. They are what they are, but nothing more than that. What they do seems to be how they are defined.

In E-Myth terms, they are technicians suffering from entrepreneurial seizures. And lots of attention is spent on them. Time spent teaching them how to organize, to market, to sell, to network, to do their bookkeeping, to get by. They are told that the idea of going out on their own is to do what they love. And once having done that, everything else will come their way.

Unfortunately, it isn't true, and it never has been. That's why most businesses fail—they aren't businesses at all. And because the people who own them, run them, and depend on them don't really love them for very long, if they ever did.

Because there is nothing to love. Unless work, for the sake of work, is something to love. Unless struggling just to make a living is something to love.

I imagine that you could make a case for it. But, I can't, and I never could. Work for the sake of work is ultimately an exhausting enterprise. All pain, no gain. Always the cart before the horse. Where's the magic, after all?

Not, mind you, that you shouldn't do what you love, if you can. But, you shouldn't attempt to build a business out of it.

More importantly, this book says that instead of doing what you love, you should love what you do. Do it and love it, provided that it makes sense, that is. Provided that there is a magnificent reason for doing it. Provided that it is much bigger than just something you love. Provided that it is something that your customers love, that your employees love, and that the community in which you do business loves. Provided that your business is a lovable, wonderful, loving thing. A remarkable, beautiful, capable, competent . . . oh well, you get my point. Love what you do, and it will love you back. And everything you put into it— your time, your energy, your money, your imagination, your sweat, your purpose, your commitment, your determination—all of that will be called a labor of love.

But, again, for all of that to happen—and it will, as you'll discover in this book—this business of yours has to make sense. And for it to make sense, for it to thrive, for it to become something much more than a job like it is now, it must possess the unique ability to grow. It must possess the unique ability to grow not just bigger, but to a substantial, unbelievable-to-you-at-this-moment-in-time size.

And that's why "10,000 times" is the First Principle. It will shape every single decision you make from the first moment you decide that a business of your own is something you truly wish to create. Or, even now, even after you've started your own business, even after you've opened the doors, even after you've set out to work like a madman or madwoman, even then, even now, we've got something big to talk about.

SOMETHING BIG TO TALK ABOUT

If it were just about size, of course, this conversation would be unnecessary. Because there's a very big part of you that believes I'm out of my mind.

You're working in your home office. Your kids are running around the house. You've just had breakfast in the kitchen nook, and your wife (or your husband) is telling the kids, "Hush! Daddy's [Mommy's] working!" And the kids react like kids do. They don't listen. Of course not. Would you? Work? What does that mean? It means whatever Mommy and Daddy do when they're not busy with you. Work makes absolutely no sense to kids. Not the kind of work you and your significant other do. If there was a tractor involved, or the horses needed to be fed, or the trees needed to be pruned, or the stone wall needed to be mended, or the car needed to be fixed, yes. Now that's work a kid can understand. It has a direct relationship with living. It's where the food comes from. It has meaning. It's real.

But, not what you do. What you do has no meaning to a kid at all. That's one reason why our kids are so distracted from the ordinary stuff of life. That's why they find so little meaning in what grownups do. And that's why, too, they find so little meaning in what you want them to do.

"To make a living? What's that?"

"Well, silly, that's where the money comes from."

"Oh."

So, the idea is (your kid thinks), that when I grow up like Mommy and Daddy, I too will end up doing things all day that haven't any meaning. So I can make a living. So I can end up old like them.

And so the reasons for this book:

- To talk about the process for creating something that has meaning. A meaning that goes beyond making a living. A meaning that goes beyond getting by. A meaning that goes beyond simply being your own boss. A meaning that goes beyond what your kids see, or what they don't.

- Something bigger. Something grander. Something more potent. Something meaningful has to happen from the very first moment you put your mind to the wheel of your imagination, or your imagination to the wheel of your mind.

- Something you can write home about.

10,000 times! Just think. What would you do if you honestly believed you were going to create 10,000 stores, 10,000 offices, 10,000 shops, or 10,000 orchards. Or 10,000 of whatever it is you have set out to do?

10,000 times! My goodness. Where in the world would you begin? And how? Let's take a look at it.

THE BEGINNING OF BIG

Everything has a beginning. That's where we are. We are going to invent an enterprise that has the ability to grow 10,000 times. We are going to do that, because if we fail to do that our enterprise won't be an enterprise; it will be incapable of growth. Don't believe me? Look at the business next door.

The business next door is easier to look at than your own. The business next door was started by Joseph, the auto mechanic. Or by Mary, the cook. Or by Frederick, the chiropractor.

But, let's for the moment stick with Joseph.

He comes to work every morning, looking pretty much the same way he looked yesterday morning, and the morning before that.

Joseph is more than likely dressed in his coveralls. They are well-worn coveralls. Probably still have the grease from yesterday's or earlier days' jobs.

On the back of his coveralls it might say something like "Joseph's Auto Repair." What else would it say? Because, of course, that's what Joseph does, and has done for years. Joseph fixes cars. Joseph has always fixed cars, either for someone else or for himself.

Joseph could be, for all you know, a fine mechanic. At least it seems like he could. Of course he may not be, but it's unlikely you'll know. There are lots of cars sitting in the lot waiting for Joseph to fix them. But, it doesn't seem to make much difference to Joseph.

People come and people go, but for all you can tell, Joseph isn't in any hurry, even though his customers seem to be. Even though his customers seem to want their car done, and done now, Joseph isn't in a hurry. But, Joseph has seen just about everything one could see when it comes to fixing cars. Cars break down. Cars get fixed. And the clock goes on, just like before.

Joseph is actually quite lucky. If predictability can be thought of as lucky, that is. Because, no matter what Joseph does or doesn't do, his business seems to continue apace, one car after another, waiting for Joseph to do what Joseph does . . . fix cars.

The clock ticks on and on. And Joseph gets older. If you could span the time, if you could see it from above; if you could watch Joseph from another perspective, see the whole story of Joseph's life, you would know something you don't know now.

Joseph long ago stopped growing. Joseph long ago went to sleep. Joseph is simply going through the motions. Joseph fixes cars. End of Joseph's story.

So, what's missing in this picture? What's missing in the picture of Joseph's Auto Repair? What's missing in the picture of Joseph's Auto Repair is something bigger than Joseph. Something bigger than work. Something bigger than making a living. Something bigger than just a job. Something alive, electric, exciting, challenging. Something that begins in the mind. Something bigger than big.

The idea of 10,000 times.

Which is where you and I are right now. We are in the idea of 10,000 times. With the very first question we are going to ask of our newly emerging company: What do you want to be when you're done? Yes, "What do you want to be when you're done?" is the biggest question we can ask of this new venture as we stand outside the door. As we begin, we see it in our imagination, in all its aspiring glory, as a work of art, a masterpiece, as a glorious system that is so stunningly effective at what it does, that it can aspire to become 10,000 times larger . . . that it can address the substance of scale.

SCALE IS THE MULTIPLICATION OF ONE

Yes, at the outset of your venture the question must be asked: "What must I do so that it can be scaled 10,000 times?"

What must I do so that every action in my company can be perfectly replicated again and again . . . 10,000 times?

What must I do so that every result in my company can be produced by 10,000 others, none of whom possesses my experience, my dedication, my skill?

Do you see the significance of these questions, my friend?

By asking these questions, you have gone beyond the province of the doer. By asking them you have entered the province of the inventor.

By pursuing them, you have awakened the true entrepreneur within.

You are now Henry Ford. Or Sam Walton. Or Michael Dell. Or Ray Kroc. Or Mary Kay. Or Anita Roddick.

This is then our conversation.

Let's look at it from the standpoint of work.

YOU ARE JOSEPH NEXT DOOR

Joseph saw 10,000 auto repair shops in his future. He thought to himself, "Why can't I do that? What is preventing me from creating a stunning enterprise of 10,000 repair shops called Joseph's? Just like Henry Ford did?"

He began, as we discussed earlier, at the beginning. To achieve that result, he will have to design a method of auto repair that is uniquely his own. Rather than simply fixing all cars, he will have to select exactly the cars that he wishes to repair. In that way, he will limit the number of options available. And by limiting the number of options available, he can direct his attention with focus. So, Joseph asked himself, "What exactly will the auto repair I do be? What is the most significant opportunity in auto repair? What do I know about the business of auto repair, its trends, where people are having the most problems, what does the research say about the most significant opportunities in auto repair?" On a hunch, Joseph asked himself, "How about green auto repair? What would green auto repair look like? What would distinguish Joseph's Green Auto from everyone else?"

And then, based only on that hunch, Joseph began to research the word "green." The ecology of automobiles. The ecology of green services. The words people were using. The frustrations people were having. The processes that could be thought of as green, as ecologically friendly, as anything and everything other than simply the words "auto repair." In short, Joseph began to think like an entrepreneur, who had size in mind, a grand result in mind, a great leap into the future in mind. He began to think of anything and everything other than simply fixing cars. He was no longer a mechanic. He was an entrepreneur.

And then the entrepreneur named Joseph thought about General Motors, Ford, and Chrysler, all of whom were closing down their dealerships and closing down their service centers. There must be an opportunity there, thought Joseph the New Entrepreneur. "And what about all the other automobile companies?" Joseph thought. "There must be something going on there that has to be interesting. And what about all the people who are losing their jobs? And what about the cost of auto repair?" As Joseph pondered these questions, he was more excited than he'd been in a long, long time. There has to be something in that muddle, Joseph thought, something waiting for me to see. 10,000 times, Joseph thought. 10,000 times an opportunity to see.

Can you feel the difference it makes thinking like new Joseph rather than like old Joseph?

Can you begin to feel what a huge difference it makes when you think 10,000 times?

Can you see that the questions you begin to ask are more provocative, less ordinary?

Can you see that these questions draw you out of your ordinary mind, and take you into places you have never gone before?

Do you see that old Joseph simply went to work?

And that going to work is exactly the opposite of what you need to do?

Do you see that going to work, as countless millions of new small business owners do, and have done for generations of start-ups, is exactly why most small businesses are doomed to not only stay small but to die small?

And there has always been another option. It's that option we are addressing here. Think 10,000 times. Think it again. Never let it leave your mind. Because in the magic of 10,000 times lies the secret of growth. And the secret of growth is your key.

Remember: If you care to, you will dare to. And nothing else will be required of you other than the will.

"The fact that I was not a trained banker and in fact had never even taken a course on bank operations meant that I was free to think about the processes of lending and borrowing without preconceptions."

—**Muhammad Yunus**
Creating a World Without Poverty

Chapter 2

The Second Principle

A Small Business Is No More Effective Than the Idea upon Which It Is Built

If most of us are ashamed of shabby clothes and shoddy furniture, let us be more ashamed of shabby ideas and shoddy philosophies. . . . It would be a sad situation if the wrapper were better than the meat wrapped inside it.

Albert Einstein

When you think back to Joseph's predicament as old Joseph, what do you see? He was thinking, first and foremost, like a mechanic. He was thinking about work and income, and how the two related to each other. He was thinking about family and kids, and about himself as a provider. He was living in the past, not in the future. Unless one could say that his past was reflected into his future and he could see nothing else.

What was also true about Joseph is that his idea was limited by his experience of himself as Joseph the mechanic. As Joseph the man who was accustomed to working for wages. As Joseph the provider. As Joseph the husband. As Joseph the father. And so his idea, the idea for his new job, working for himself—what we all call his business—was a pure reflection of his old job and his old mind-set. He was a worker for wages, and the wages are earned by doing what he knows how to do. He started his business, and paid himself, rather than an employer paying him. Nothing much had changed. He still worked hard, but now had "other work" to do as well—necessary work, heartless work, mundane work.

But, now, Joseph, miracle upon miracle, is thinking "10,000 times!" Joseph is open to the possibility of a new idea. His new idea started out as the word "green." Simply that. No idea how THAT came into his mind, but it did, just like that. It was stimulated, as his mind was, by the *other* idea, called "10,000 times." But, that was only the first idea that came into his mind.

The second idea that came into Joseph's mind was the idea related to General Motors, Ford, and Chrysler, and the alarming fact that they were all closing down dealerships, scaling down, which meant they were also closing down service centers.

This also meant that jobs were being lost, in massive numbers. And jobs were being lost not only at General Motors, Ford, and Chrysler but also in all the other major companies whose livelihood was stricken by the enormity of the financial collapse of the general market, called Wall Street, and banks, and financial services companies, and insurance companies, and the like.

How could so many smart guys go so wrong?

Now, new Joseph—not the old Joseph we've known from the past—is looking around himself as if for the very first time, thinking about circumstances and conditions and economics, for goodness sake. Joseph had never had an economic thought in his head before, other than the ones directly related to the income he produced, to his work, and to his job.

And Joseph was thinking about his family. Joseph was not what one would consider to be a political sort of man. Oh, sure, he voted, but not so much so that it made a dent in the way he thought about things. But now he was thinking about his country. He was thinking about life in general. He was thinking as never before, other than with a bit of complaining from time to time. But, everyone did that, didn't they? Of course, Joseph would tell you.

He has always been a fairly predictable guy. But not now! This amazingly un-Joseph–like thought of 10,000 times! "Where in the world did *that* come from?" Joseph wondered.

And now . . . given the first thought, and the second thought, and the third thought . . . given the remarkable open space in his mind, a space seemed to appear on its own, for all the reasons Joseph could never share with you. Given that space in his mind, an entire avalanche of new thoughts began to flow from inside Joseph to his rapidly eager and hungry mind, as though to fill that space. But, of greatest surprise to Joseph, the space was not only *not* being filled—it was seemingly unfillable!

The next thought that came to Joseph was about doing something other than auto repair. What about all those folks whose incomes and livelihoods were being shattered by the economic debacle that pressed upon their lives and communities? What would they do with their cars? How could they afford to have them fixed or serviced at the increasingly expensive rates he knew only so well? After all, he was charging them!

A mechanic, for goodness sake, thought Joseph for the very first time — charging out at more than $100 an hour! Who would have thought? Certainly not old Joseph years ago when he was employed by others. He never gave it a thought what his time was billed out as by "the boss." He got paid what he got paid, and it was never enough. And that's why he decided to go out on his own. To get paid what he was worth, or at least what the market told him he was worth. And to hell with the customer! This was how the world worked after all.

If you could bill yourself out at $100 an hour (as a mechanic, for goodness sake!), you would be a *fool* to work for anything less. "Look at what doctors are paid," old Joseph had thought. "Look at electricians," he thought, when he had to have one come to his home to fix a circuit breaker that he couldn't, for whatever reason, fix himself.

"What's the opportunity in all that?" new Joseph asked, suddenly seeing the world from the other side. Suddenly he realized that people's pain was a message that he shouldn't ignore. Every one of the catastrophes underway bore a message for him on an entrepreneurial scale. And that's when his next idea came to mind.

What about creating a business that teaches people how to fix their own cars? What about teaching people to fix their cars at a mere fraction of the cost of having him, Joseph, fix their cars? What if he were to do that? And how *would* he do that, Joseph wondered next? How could he possibly teach people who didn't know anything about cars to do it themselves?

"How would that work?" he thought, with the increasing complexity of autos today?

"Impossible," he thought.

But . . . what if he could? The next thoughts followed on the heels of impossible. How would he, if he did?

HOW WOULD HE? HOW WOULD YOU?

If the idea for your business is simply about work and income, then your business will suffer just like you.

It will stress and it will strain.

It will get ugly and tired and cynical.

It will be a victim to all the customer abuses you experience, and it will not act kindly to any of them.

If your idea for your business is simply about work and income, then your business will lack imagination and become resentful and fearful and exhausted.

It will produce stories to tell at night to the kids or anyone who will listen about how unfair the world is, and how ridiculous big companies are, and how good people aren't appreciated like they should be—like *you* should be—and what a dismal world it is.

If your idea for your business is about working for a living, then your business will end up working for a living. And it will persist in working for a living. But in the end, never will it really create the kind of living you believe you deserve. Your business will become old and tired and run down, not spotless like you kept it at the very beginning when you opened its doors. That beginning, when you were so optimistic, so incredibly excited, so independent, so young, will be a worn and faded memory.

Change that idea! Now! If you want to change your business, change the idea of your business, or forever hold your peace.

THAT'S THE BEGINNING OF THIS PICTURE

Joseph was excited. The idea of 10,000 times changed the pictures he saw. He told his wife about it. He wrote notes to himself about it. He found himself talking to himself about it, at the least likely times: in the bathroom, in the bedroom, under a car as he worked. He would stop in the middle of whatever he was doing and, if he forgot to bring a piece of paper and a pencil with him, he would immediately try to save it in his mind.

But then the idea would get lost, and he would be frantic, because he knew that the idea that came to him in that moment was so precious. "I've got to remember to bring a pad of paper with me wherever I go," new Joseph thought to himself. I must absolutely remember. And so he got a small notebook to record his thoughts.

He was determined. He made a promise to himself not to forget it, but then he did forget it. He couldn't remember for the life of him how he forgot it, but he did. And then he would remonstrate with himself, in this undertow of conversation between old Joseph and new Joseph that something important was being lost if he failed to remember to do this one thing: to bring a notebook and pencil with him wherever he went. "You must do that," new Joseph said to old Joseph. "You must!"

And old Joseph would listen with half of his head, and even less of his heart. He would hear new Joseph talking to him, but he could not fathom what it was all about. And the tussle between the two continued day and night.

THE AGGRAVATION OF AN IDEA

Yes, an idea is aggravating. It demands that you do something about it. It speaks in tones unaccustomed to the old mind. The old mind—old Joseph's mind—your old mind—is not accustomed to thinking in such aggravated ways. Ideas, especially new ideas, are aggravating. They challenge your old mind to leave and make room for your new mind. This is not so easily done. Because, for your old mind to finally leave means that your old mind is dead. Old minds don't die easily. No, they don't! They are not very good "diers." They want to live, like all of us do. And yet, for the idea, the new idea, to be born, it must come from inside of you. It must come from a stimulated state of being. It must come from the new you, not the old you. It must be radiant, and extravagantly so. It must sing of soul, of soul music, of desire, of depth, of a hunger that has no limits. It does not sing of a hunger for more stuff. Goodness no. It must be born of a hunger to touch something you haven't touched, to feel something you haven't felt, to love something you haven't loved, to serve something you haven't served.

All ideas are aggravating.

They punish us with their insistence of being heard. They challenge us with their insistence of being nurtured. They stimulate us beyond our ability to feel that much, to do that much, to go that far. All ideas are aggravating because they won't quit being ideas. They are the exacerbation of intellect, the exaggeration of form and color, the conflagration of energy, of both the old and the new. They travel in loud voices, hanging on to the handholds of the unfamiliar carriage that your emotional horse is pulling. "Stop pulling me," your old self says. "Stop talking to me," your old self complains. "Stop activating me," even your new self shouts, feeling even as he or she is creating this, that what has been created has a life of its own.

10,000 times! What an exaggerated state of being! Who needs to do that much? Who can even stretch that far? Is that not simply hyperbole? Simply excess?

"Well, no, not in the least," the new mind says. But what is the idea worthy of that growth? Not the one you've got in your head. Not just anything waiting to be done. But, *something* waiting to be done. Something quite miraculous, if indeed it could be done.

SOMETHING MIRACULOUS, IF INDEED IT COULD BE DONE

Joseph went walking for hours—early in the morning, late at night. Joseph's new mind went walking, not for the exercise, oh no. His mind went walking for the movement of it. The movement of it cleaned out the new cobwebs that were different from the old. New cobwebs formed just like old cobwebs did. The spider did his work as his nature told him to. The spider connected the parts of the picture together without any understanding, other than that is what spiders do. The new cobwebs were actually quite different from the old, in that they were born of a new energy in new Joseph's new mind. They weren't about work. They weren't about the pragmatics of old Joseph's life. They weren't about getting things done because that's what needed to be done. They were about exploration. They were about stretching from one limb to the next, to see what would happen when the connection was made . . . There was the flavor of reaching, of stretching, of something far beyond what spiders are interested in doing. This was a very human web. This was a web of discovery . . . a web of confusion . . . a web of intrigue.

Old Joseph would look at himself and wonder whether he had lost his mind. And of course the answer was always very clear. That yes, he had lost his mind. And yet, there was nothing he wanted to do about it.

A *small business is only as effective as the idea upon which it is built.*

What's your idea? What's your new business going to look like when it's finally, finally done? What is miraculous if indeed it could be done?

THE CREATION OF AN IDEA

So, by this time you understand that the idea is not simply something that arrives unbidden in a gift box packaged by someone else. You do realize that, don't you?

You realize that Joseph had to undergo a major transition. Better yet, it was a transformation. It was a transformation from the old to the new. And that the new was not simply the old in different clothes. The new was just that . . . *new.*

Old Joseph could never, not in his entire lifetime, create the idea upon which new Joseph's life would be rebuilt. Old Joseph lived by rules that prohibited aggravated dreaming. Old Joseph's rules, while they served old Joseph's life, were unfitting for a life upon which new Joseph's being was to be founded. All of that must be obvious to you by now.

So, then, the question remains, how and where and when is this all encompassing new idea born? Follow me here. This could be challenging if you're not available.

The new idea, the very one we are looking for here, is born the same way that you were born. Your soul, resting in the ether of the universe, was stimulated by a conception here on Earth. Two lovers touched each other and their voice, the one voice made of the two voices, called out to you, that soul I speak of, that soul who was waiting in the sphere of awakening, in the universal sphere, in the timeless warp of eternal remembering. An idea is also born in the ether of the universe. The idea we are speaking of here is born either of lust or of love. But, in either case, it is born again, not for the first time. It is born again. Of that I can assure you. How I know that is not the question, even though you may be asking it. That I know that is the key to the fact that you know that too. An idea is very simply said, born.

And when an idea is born, you are born again too.

A small business is no bigger than the idea upon which it was born.

Remember this notion. That is the point of the Second Principle.

As for me, I have a condominium with a view of the Golden Gate Bridge and sufficient cash to indulge in pleasures you might think superfluous. But remember that when we met I was mired in student loans, compared to me you were born to have a restless conscience, and to act on it. Still I question myself every time I imagine you asking, "Is this a life of meaning?" Then I imagine the conveyor belt of life leading straight to my premature demise, keeling over at my desk on another weekend of too much work for no great cause. Perhaps that's why I spend so much time at the gym.

—Richard North Patterson
Eclipse

Chapter 3

The Third Principle

A Small Business Is a System in Which All Parts Contribute to the Success or Failure of the Whole

Of all the things I've done, the most vital is coordinating those who work with me and aiming their efforts at a certain goal.
—Walt Disney

Let's revisit where we've been and where we are. The small business you are inventing as the Most Successful Small Business in the World will not be small at all. It will be perfectly mirrored in its 10,000th clone. It will be built to perfection—or as we said, "rightly"—in its first iteration, the small business prototype that is then ready to be replicated 10,000 times. It may be just like the business you have right now, but this one will be created with a completely fresh and original mind (your new mind, not your old mind), to manifest itself as an idea worthy of growth. This idea will stand apart from income and work. This idea will stimulate the new mind in a way the old mind could never be stimulated. The idea, the great idea, the highly differentiated idea, the idea that fulfills a need in a way that has never been exactly fulfilled before, is the core conceptual framework upon which your most successful small business will be built.

Now we are confronted by the Third Principle: that a small business is a system in which all parts contribute to the success or failure of the whole.

This means that Joseph must apply his new mind to more than what he knows. He must apply it to doing the job at hand. He must calibrate the parts of the entire system, through which results are produced, in and by the company he is inventing. But this is more than calibration. It is collaboration of parts. This speaks to something he has never thought about before.

A COLLABORATION OF PARTS

In every task, in each of the components of the machinery, and outside of it, there is a connection that must be understood. Like Henry Ford, Joseph will design an original methodology that produces an original result, differentiating his company, his small business, his product. To do this, he must understand the connection of the parts. Like Henry Ford understood the Ford Motor Car and the Ford Motor Company, which manufactures, sells, and services the car, Joseph must understand the connection of parts in his business, and how his company relates to the world.

All parts of this system must be identified, taken apart (so to speak), and then reassembled in a way to collectively and collaboratively function in the production of a finer result than was previously possible.

Joseph must do this. As you must do this. And he must begin this before he goes to work on his business. He must start the beginning of his new venture with a completely new mind. He must understand that the original nature of his new work is the critical key to creating the brand—the Ford Motor Car and Company—of his particular choosing.

So where to begin?

You begin with this: Know that the system is a collaboration of parts. The parts of the system follow:

1. Parts outside of the business:
   a. Consumer parts
   b. Competitor parts
   c. Channels of distribution parts
   d. Media parts
   e. Financial parts
2. Parts inside of the business:
   a. Strategic parts
   b. Tactical parts
   c. Incremental parts

What does all of this mean?

- It means that the system is first focused outside of the business, rather than inside of the business.

- It means that the system is first focused on the customer, then the competitor, then the channel of distribution, then the channel of communication (the media), and finally the sources of capital (the financial aspects).

- It means that the idea of the business is more important than the work of the business.

- It means exactly the opposite of what old Joseph would have thought.

- It is counterintuitive to the approach that most small business owners take when thinking about, and then launching, their new business.

All small business owners start with what *they* want and move out from there.

That is an old-minded approach.

All new-minded entrepreneurs start on the outside of the business, in the mind and soul and heart and life of the customer they intend to serve. That is where the idea is born, the same idea that will transform your chosen customer's life.

And it is only there, where the idea takes form as an integrated system that this idea becomes more than an ephemeral vision. It becomes a transformational fact. This fact possesses the energy and the capability to grow itself as many times as it chooses to—10,000 times . . . and even more.

IDENTIFYING THE PARTS

Let's review the parts as we defined them. The parts that need to be addressed outside of your business follow:

1. **Customer Parts:** Later in this chapter I have included a model that I call the Consumer Identification Startup Matrix to assist you in the process of identifying your most important customer by first looking at the challenges he or she faces in life. Once having identified the challenges, you can then determine how you intend to resolve those challenges. In Joseph's case, we have already begun that task by becoming aware of the economic devastation that is occurring all around him, including in the automobile and transportation industries. Because Joseph's life has been spent working as a mechanic in the automobile industry, he has an ability to see it from a worker's perspective. Add to that his new mind—that of an entrepreneur—and suddenly his old mind can inform his new mind with experience that his new mind wouldn't have. Combine his experience *inside* the industry with his newfound interest from *outside* the industry and you have the makings of a new partnership that could add power to his new insights, and add leverage to his old experience. To move your thoughts forward, go to the Consumer Identification Startup Matrix at the end of the chapter.

2. **Competitor Parts:** Every customer is being pursued by a competitor of the company you intend to create. Each of those competitors is offering alternative solutions to your chosen customer's concerns, frustrations, and needs. Your job is to identify each of those competitors, categorize them by the offer they make; the method they use to make that offer; the effectiveness of

their solution to the particular problem that their company and products were designed to serve; the media they use; the messages they send; the positioning they have adopted in the customers' mind—such as better, faster, cheaper, or unique; the channels of distribution that they have elected to utilize; the price point of their products or services; size of the business; how long they have been in business; the rate of their growth; and the success of their offer. Each of the above is a part. Each needs to be added to your spectrum of parts to begin to see how all these parts can potentially collaborate with each other.

3. **Channels of Distribution Parts:** There is a vast array of channels of distribution to choose from, but only some of them may be effective. Some of these channels are the Internet, and all of the various formats utilizing the Internet; direct selling through your own direct sales force; direct selling through large existing networks; direct selling through small independent sales reps; franchises through your own franchise system; franchises through large existing franchise systems; franchising through small independent systems; retailing through your own stores; retailing through large existing chain stores; retailing through small existing independent stores; wholesaling; cable TV; public TV; large TV networks; small, independent TV networks; self-publishing; large publishers; small, independent, specialized publishers; your own services; large chain services; small independent service companies; your own network marketing; large marketing networks; small, independent marketing networks; licensing your own network; licensing via large existing manufacturers; and licensing via small independent manufacturers. Your selection of distribution channels may include any number of the above, or only one, or a few of these choices. Above all, the channels you choose will determine your reach, and its cost,

effectiveness, and limitations. In other words, should you choose to distribute your product or service through an infomercial on cable TV, that might exclude many other opportunities that you could have included, for example if you're selling your books through book stores, they would be adverse to your selling the same book (or giving it away) on an infomercial. Remember that a collaboration of the parts is essential when it comes to distribution.

4. **Media Parts:** Remember Marshall McLuhan's thesis, "the medium is the message"? "The message is the medium" as well. And the medium of the message is called the media. One form of the media includes newspapers (local); newspapers (regional); newspapers (national). There are two forms of media available in the newspapers: news and advertising. News is either straightforward, where you have done something in your company, or with your company, that is news worthy, or news is the less straightforward kind, called publicity. The second form of media in newspapers is advertising. That's where you buy space to sell your product, your service, your company. Advertising done well can also be disguised as news: local magazines; regional magazines; national magazines; trade magazines; industry-specific magazines; topic-specific magazines; market-specific magazines; reader-specific magazines; TV advertising of all kinds (see in distribution); pay-per-lead TV; pay-per-sale TV; TV news; TV publicity; TV infomercial; your own TV show; sponsor for someone else's TV show; Internet radio; AM radio; public radio; all versions listed under TV are also available through radio; Internet (all of the above and more); your own CDs; someone else's CDs; your own DVDs; someone else's DVDs; your own books; and someone else's books. The options and variety of options with media are extremely variable. You can use every kind of media and in every mixture of media. You can do that

expensively, or you can do that inexpensively. Inexpensively is best, because, as with all industries today, media is experiencing a horrendous crunch. What once worked with little thought, no longer works so well, even with a great deal of thought. But, the message still is the medium, no matter what's going on outside, and the medium still is the message: Get yourself out there as well, as often as you can.

5. **Financial Parts:** This has to do with capitalizing your new venture, the Most Successful Small Business in the World. There's good and bad news here. I tend to focus on the good news: Once you get to the point of launch, because the model for your new business starts out very small—remember, this is called the Most Successful Small Business in the World—while you're proving your concept, designing your idea, and building your prototype, much of what you need to do will be self-funded. That means help comes from friends and family and from people who know you but who also trust you. If they don't help, it will be a little more difficult, but still doable. This is the first part of the financial parts: bootstrapping. Let's make a list then. The financial parts are bootstrapping (called "find it where you find it, get it where you can"); venture capitalists; angels; other successful entrepreneurs in the industry you're pursuing; other successful entrepreneurs in industries compatible with the one you're pursuing; successful manufacturers in the industry you're pursuing as strategic partners/investors; successful service companies in the industry you're pursuing as strategic partners/investors; successful retailers in the industry you're pursuing, who are not competitive with you, as strategic partners/investors; successful distributors in the industry you're pursuing, noncompetitive with you, who could become suppliers for you as strategic partners/investors; unsuccessful competitors in the industry you're pursuing, who would be open to being acquired, as strategic partners/

investors; successful advertisers to the industry you're pursuing as strategic partners/investors; successful network marketing companies within the industry you're pursuing as strategic partners/investors. Remember, each and every part of the system on the outside of your business must collaborate with each and every other part of the system for the whole system to work synergistically. This collaboration must occur for the system to become the Most Successful Small Business in the World. So, putting the pieces together as we said and say at E-Myth, is the key to organizing your new company for growth.

Now let's look at the parts *inside* of your business.

There are three such parts:

- The strategic parts

- The tactical parts

- And the incremental parts

The strategic parts that need to be addressed *inside* of your business are:

1. Strategy

2. Marketing

3. Operations

4. Finance

Your CEO is your chief strategist.
Your CMO is your chief marketer.
Your COO is your chief organizer.
Your CFO is your chief financial officer.

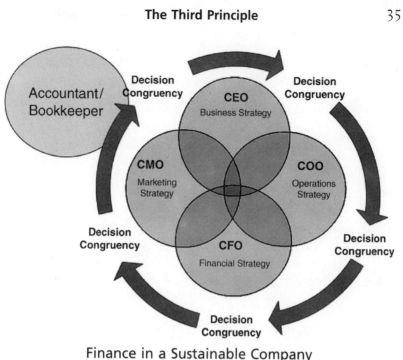

Finance in a Sustainable Company

Strategy. Marketing. Operations. Finance. The four essential functions of the Most Successful Small Business in the World. They work in tandem as a strategic team.

Let's take a closer look at each strategic part.

The Strategic Parts

Strategic Parts of Strategy (CEO's Accountability)

- Idea: The dream.

- Vision: How it will be organized.

- Purpose: Its main reason for being, and for whom.

- Mission: The primary development that needs to be done, all combining (collaborating) to tell the story of your business, including:

Whom it serves.

Why it serves them.

How it serves them.

Why it is essential to them.

How it transforms them.

What it pragmatically provides to them.

How it pragmatically provides it to them.

At what price it provides it to them.

At what profit it provides it to them.

How they can afford it.

What differentiates you and what you do from every other alternative.

Why that differentiation will survive over time.

Strategic Parts of Marketing (CMO's Accountability)

- Consumer selection
- Positioning (ours in relationship to theirs)
- Packaging (we look like this, because—color, shape, form)
- Product/service design (look at Apple—that says it all)

- Language to define (this is the description of why we did this)

- Language to describe (this is the description of how it works)

- Language to broadcast (this is the announcement of news about our breakthrough)

- Language to educate (this is the education of the customer— what happened to cause the problem we're solving, and how that has affected you)

- Distribution

- Competitor analysis and assessment

- Sales and selling (the system for, the justification for, the organization of)

- Advertising

- Company packaging (the look, the feel, the emotional impact, the functional predictability, the brand, the brand, the brand, the brand . . . we could go on and on)

- And, finally, about the markets we serve, where they are, where they are going, who else is going there, and how we will fare in relationship with all of the above

Strategic Parts of Operations (COO's Accountability)

- Execution of the plan

- Design of the organization

- Delivery of the brand

- Fulfillment of the promise

- Congruence to standards

- Impeccability of the team

- Consistency (no compromise, no excuses)

- If a swat team is good, then this team is called triple swat

- Creation of the operating system

- Flawless execution

- 10,000 mind-set (performed to a tee)

- One small business at a time

- Documentation and orchestration of all actions to a tee

- The system is the solution. And the system is doing much, much better than well. And where it isn't, we're on it. And when we're on it, it's done!

Strategic Parts of Finance (CFO's Accountability)

- Capital when needed, and no sooner

- Quantification of performance to a tee

- Reporting of all required performance indicators, on time, every time, exactly when needed

- All financial relationships (holding to a standard)

- Communication with all financial partners on a consistent, preplanned basis

- Honor of all financial commitments, on time, as promised, exactly as needed

- Communication with all managers about what they need to know about performance, capital requirements, cash flow, and profitability

- Financial information about competitors, about the markets we serve, and about the general market as a whole

The Tactical Parts

Tactical Parts of Strategy (CEO's Accountability)

- Marketing
- Operations
- Finance

Tactical Parts of Marketing (CMO's Accountability and Respective Managers' Responsibility)

- Sales
- Copywriting
- Graphic design
- Product design
- Publicity
- Public relations
- Webmaster
- Internet as media

- Internet as marketing communications

- Internet as product fulfillment

- Internet as sales

Tactical Parts of Operations (COO's Accountability and Respective Managers' Responsibility)

- Production

- Client fulfillment

- Internet

- Operational reporting to senior managers

- Operational reporting to all stores

- Operational reporting to standards

- Operation of the Internet

- Systems development

- Systems monitoring

Tactical Parts of Finance (CFO's Accountability and Respective Managers' Responsibility)

- Accounting

- Accounts payable

- Accounts receivable

- Cash flow management and reporting

- Balance sheet

- Reports to the stores

- Reports from the stores

- Store financial operations

- Corporate financial operations

- Financial reports to senior management

- Management of the financial plan

- Reports to the financial market

The Incremental Parts

Incremental Parts of Tactics

All the work done by each technician in each of the categories listed previously under tactical parts: In each case, what is done is called *tactical work*.

A SUMMARY OF THE PARTS

See each of the parts listed, from the first to the last. See that each of those parts must collaborate with each of the other parts to form a whole. See that until and unless each of those parts fits in a collaborative, highly systemic way with each of the other parts— *with each and every one of them!*—discord will be the order of the day.

You cannot and will not—will *never*—build the Most Successful Small Business in the World out of discord. This little beastie will not fly.

Yes, when it comes to the Most Successful Small Business in the World, order is the order of the day.

And order calls for symmetry. And symmetry calls for balance. And balance calls for consistency. And consistency calls for integration. And integration calls for parts that fit together as the parts of a well-hewn puzzle do.

See the picture. See the picture completed. See the picture telling the completed story. See it in your mind. See the picture in you.

Consumer Identification Startup Matrix

Age Groups	Area of Need	Fulfillment
Newborn 0–1 month	Care	**Health:** Nursing or caregiving that specializes in newborns, new technology that better diagnoses newborn issues **Hygiene:** Improved filtering and ventilation systems, improved sanitation procedures, natural bed clothing and blankets, improved baby monitoring equipment **Diapers:** Better-designed diapers for comfort and leaks, diapers with sensors, diapers that dissolve in landfills quickly **Crying:** Creation of soothing devices, vibrating/rocking beds, activated recordings of mother's voice
Prenatal through newborn 0–1 month	Heath issues	**Deformity/retardation:** Education for pregnant women about causes of deformities and other complications, medicines for prevention; high-impact nutrition for expecting mothers; rehab for alcohol- or other drug-addicted mothers; testing for genetics and health issues

		Sudden death syndrome: Comfortable device that monitors baby vitals, alarm system, cribs that jolt when breathing stops
Newborn 0–1 month	Adoption	**Adoption:** Affordable, efficient, well-screened adoption programs; nationwide database for foster and adoptive parents
Newborn 0–1 month through infant	Nutrition	**Breastfeeding:** New ways to pump and store milk, testing of breast milk, better cover-ups so that mothers can breastfeed in public, education for new moms about the benefits of breast milk **Solids:** Super-concentrated nutritional foods, natural baby foods and drinks, sugar-free snacks, meal plans, food delivery service, self-service meal preparation/classes
Infant through toddler	Day care/babysitting	**Day care/babysitting:** Certification for qualified child care, parental alerts, spyware to watch babysitter, rules and guidelines, manuals on do's and don'ts, guidelines for hiring a babysitter
Infant through toddler	Development	**Walking:** Device that helps kids stand up **Talking:** Recording devices that can pronounce words while parent is not present **Toilet training:** Teaching tools, teaching toys, kid toilets **Toys:** Interactive, educational, fun, engaging, teaching tool, safe
Infant through toddler	Safety	**Child abduction:** Child monitors, programs such as amber alerts, GPS units for children, child's jewelry connected to

(*Continued*)

(Continued)

		parent's alert system; billboards that can be turned into pictures of missing child-systems that perform immediate lockdown
Child age 4–13 years	Learning	**Learning:** Knowledge/understanding the world **School:** Keeping kids interested, new ways of approaching class time, new approaches to student–teacher interactions **Manners:** Table manners, phone/email etiquette, introductions, consideration of others
Child age 4–13 years	Safety/social development	**Safety:** Self-defense classes **Character training:** Workbooks, programs, classes on character **Mentoring:** Positive role model programs, after-school programs, theater programs, life skills training programs **Too much television:** Timers that shut down television after specified period, parental controls, exercise units that power the TV, such as peddling or walking
Child age 4–13 years	Transportation	Services to get kids back and forth to school, getting kids to extracurricular activities, matching children with similar interests.
Child age 4–13 years	Health issues	**Obesity:** Education, exercise trainers for youth, parental education, early habit development, awareness campaigns, exercise classes in school, healthier nutrition in schools

		Abuse: More runaway shelters for kids; more incentives for foster parents; programs in which runaways can get an education, financial help, medical help
Teenagers	Social development	**Anxiety/drama:** Teaching goal setting so that energy is focused, teaching meditation and breathing techniques to teens, teaching about different personalities to decrease drama and increase tolerance **Internet:** Teaching Internet etiquette, privacy, digital tattoos
Teenagers	Health and safety	**Diet:** Cooking programs for healthy eating **Acne:** Access to effective medications, providing widespread information on skin care, teaching the effects of diet and lifestyle choices on skin **Safety:** Pepper spray, self-defense classes **Drugs/alcohol:** Recovery centers, interventions, education, parental controls, alternative activities **Running away from home:** Shelters for kids, foster programs
Teenagers	College/career	**College/career:** "First job" program, availability for more affordable classes, alternative schools/classroom settings, more disciplined classroom environments, separate the kids who want to learn from those who don't **Career:** Regional occupation programs (ROPs), showing teens the components of different jobs, job training in high school, dissipating gender roles in occupations; innovative education programs for single gender; training for tutor programs;

(Continued)

(Continued)

		innovative driving course; high-adventure programs
Middle age	Aging, finance	**Aging:** Advanced wrinkle serums, super nutrition-packed foods, anti-aging nutrients **Weight:** Low-fat and low-sugar snacks, scales, weight-loss clinics **Disease:** Better medicine, new diagnosis techniques **Family:** New devices to communicate and stay connected **Loss:** Grief counseling and classes **Image:** Better social skills **Depression:** Medicines, better ways to diagnose, expand awareness campaigns **Caretaker:** More certified caretaking training, innovative, and convenient programs for parents **Finances:** Simpler investment programs, education for women in managing money **Debt:** Debt relief programs, lenders, money management, retirement planning
Mature adult	Family, health, safety	**Widowed:** Grief classes, support groups **Caregiving:** More certified caretaking training, screening techniques, back-ground checks, video monitoring, nationwide networking **Safety:** Security services, safe home design **Finances:** Pooling finances with family and friends, cohabitating, splitting costs, insurance services

		Health/longevity: Coping skills, nutritional products, dental care, medicines, surgeries, skin treatments, memory enhancers, doctor monitoring **Retirement:** Community activities, social security, cost sharing, downsizing, minimal living, travel **Lifestyle:** Staying active, flexibility, exercise
Elderly	Caregiving, finance, end-of-life issues	**Caregiving:** Certified caretaking training, screening techniques, background checks, video monitoring, nationwide networking **Safety:** Security services, safe home design **Family:** Help for families with dependent parents, services that deliver meals and meds, shoppers and errand runner service **Widowed/loss:** Grief classes, support networks, funeral services, burial services, end-of-life issues **Finances:** Counseling, pooling finances with family and friends, cohabitating, splitting costs, insurance services **Nutrition:** Easy-to-consume nutritional supplements **Life expectancy/longevity:** Supplements **Mental decline/memory loss:** Testing equipment, memory exercises **Purpose:** More social acceptance of aging, productive and worthwhile work, improving perception of aging

it came to me suddenly, even
without a thought.
not anticipated, but suddenly
a realization
that my life, the rest of it
I mean
could be
much different than
the beginning of it
or at least what
it has come to
at this point in time.
it came to me suddenly,
so clear, so complete
that it surprised me how
little of it I had
appreciated.

—Michael E. Gerber

Chapter 4

The Fourth Principle

A Small Business Must Be Sustainable Through All Economic Conditions, in All Markets, Providing Meaningful, Highly Differentiated Results to All of Its Customers

The beautiful rests on the foundations of the necessary.
—Ralph Waldo Emerson

How in the world can one predict economic conditions for our Most Successful Small Business in the World, readers ask me, when we've just witnessed the most dire, disastrous, absurd, and tragic financial debacle of all time? Yes, even worse than the Great Depression!

Aren't you tired of hearing that weary expression? Who today even *remembers* the Great Depression? Who even *cares* to remember it? Back then, when all the businesses died? Back then, when millions upon millions of desperate, hopeless people stood in long lines—*in the USA!*—waiting for food, waiting for work that wasn't going to come? My father lived during that time, and my mother did as well, but neither my father nor my mother ever talked about it.

And what are we saying when we consider all that? I think we're all saying the very same thing . . . How could so many presumably smart people make such obviously foolish decisions in these sumptuous days of such plenty?

Foolish? Hell! Their decisions were far worse than that!

You can put reason to foolish. But, stupid? No. Stupid is as stupid does, somebody said in a movie not that long ago.

Stupid is unkind, in fact, when looking at not only what has happened over the past five years, but at what's continuing to happen even now. No, it's a bit uglier than that. Much, much uglier. Ugly is as ugly does. *I'm* stupid. *They* are not stupid. They are narcissistic serial criminals who should be locked up for the rest of their lives for the destruction that they created.

So, back to the original thought: *A small business must be sustainable through all economic conditions.*

If all of those financial experts, all of those financial advisors, all of those coaches, and mentors, and leaders, and lenders, didn't know what was going on, how could you or I possibly invent the Most Successful Small Business in the World given standards like: *must be sustainable through all economic conditions?*

How indeed?

Well, the answer is easy. Apply and obey the Ten Principles!

Had Enron applied and obeyed the Ten Principles, it would still be here today.

If Arthur Anderson had applied and obeyed the Ten Principles, it would still be here today. *Arthur Anderson!* Can you believe that?

If the largest mortgage lenders in the world had applied and obeyed the Ten Principles, there would be absolutely no question but that they would still be here today and the mortgage industry would be thriving.

If the largest financial services firms like AIG had applied and obeyed the Ten Principles, they would not be suffering to the degree that they (and we along with them) are suffering today.

There is nothing more fundamental to the creation and growth of an economically sound company than The Ten Principles. They cannot fail you. They cannot fail, no matter what the economic conditions surrounding you are.

Let's look at some of the fundamentals.

THE FUNDAMENTALS OF SUCCESS

There are seven fundamental rules for the selection, design, building, and growth of the Most Successful Small Business in the World.

Rule #1: Choose the Most Ordinary

What do I mean by the most ordinary? I mean to make and sell those products and services that will never go out of fashion: food, health care, clothing, communication, transportation, comfort, to name but a few. Do I mean to say that you can't fail in any of those categories? Of course not; many, and indeed most, do. But, they won't fail if they apply and obey the Ten Principles. What I do mean to say is to do only those things that will not go out of fashion. Fashion is unpredictable. Fashion changes overnight. Fashion is whimsy. Great companies aren't unpredictable or whimsical. Great companies are rock solid. They are fundamental. They do only what tradition expects them to do. They do what longevity expects them to do, what necessity tells them to do. Do what is necessary, this rule says. Does that mean that such companies don't innovate? Of course not. Innovation is not fashion; innovation is invention. Innovation of the ordinary creates the extraordinary, but in an ordinary frame of mind. Find a better way to do a basic thing. Find a better way to do the ordinary: to feed people, to clothe people, to house people, to move people, to create wellness for people . . . to do all those things people need companies to do. Do these things and your company will thrive.

Rule #2: Constantly Improve

Companies die because they choose to do the wrong things, yes, but mainly they die because they choose to remain static. Tradition isn't static. Tradition is consistent. Companies that remain static refuse to thrive. They are hanging on to the past, not creating it. That's right, great companies are continually re-creating the past. Today is the past tomorrow. Tomorrow is the past, the day after. Great companies are continually establishing the standards for everyone else, because they are committed to standards. They are committed to doing elemental things, essential things, better than anyone else does them. They do this without forgetting what is elemental, without forgetting what is essential. The Most Successful Small Business in the World will become so because it is constantly improving not only what it does but how it does it. Had General Motors followed its own rules, it would still be the great company it once was. If General Motors had continued to improve, it would still be leading the auto industry today, as it had from the outset. But it failed to improve. It failed to improve the results it delivered to its customers. This is what business is always about: results. In *The E-Myth* I said, "Focus on Results. Not on Work." Constantly improve your results.

Rule #3: Listen to Your Customer

Yes, I know, everyone says this—"Listen to your customer"—but so few actually do it. What does it mean to listen to your customer? It means to watch her. Follow her. Hear what she says. See what she does. It means to understand how it feels to be her. Know what she thinks about herself when she gets up in the morning. When she feeds the kids. When she gets dressed and goes to work. When she does what she does. When she goes to lunch. When she comes back and when she takes a break in the afternoon. What does she do when she's finished at work? How does it feel to be her when she comes home? What does home look like? How clean is it? How organized is it? How is it furnished? What does she do when she comes home? Does she watch TV? Does she take care of the kids' dinner? Does she have kids? How old are her kids? What are they doing all day? Do they go to school? Are they good students? Do they have problems at school? And on and on and on. Listen to your customer. Know who she is, what she does, what she prefers to do. Pay attention to your customer. Get to know her better than you know yourself.

Rule #4: Respond to What You Hear, See, and Feel

Just listening to your customer—seeing her, feeling her, following her, paying attention to her—is a waste of time and money if you are not building your responses to her into the nuts and bolts of your company. The nuts and bolts of your company are conceived, designed, constructed, and conveyed in the framework of your company; in the culture of your company; in the deliverables of your company; in the heart, soul, and sensibilities of your company; in everything it does and will do. There must be a mechanism in place for this to occur on a daily, ritualized basis. There must be a system. Your people must live and breathe this system. They must understand and convey this system. They must see and feel and display this system to each other and all of your company's partners, suppliers, and investors. Your company will be known as the company that does what your company does. It will become your badge of honor. It is the identification key that says your company's name, where your company's name will be shared, spoken of, and, yes, revered, as the most unusual company they have ever seen or heard of. It's the stuff that makes the Most Successful Small Business in the World exactly that. It's the stuff that's missing in all other companies that have no idea of the power of that stuff. In short, your company does what other companies have no idea needs to be done.

Remember it. If you don't, your company will most certainly forget it.

Rule #5: Set the Highest Standards

When I speak of the Most Successful Small Business in the World, I am speaking of exactly that. That means there is no one better. It means that your standards become the benchmark for all other companies' standards. That doesn't mean that you emulate others; it means that they emulate you. Your standards therefore need to be so high that no other company can hope to emulate them in the near term. And because you are constantly improving, they would be hard pressed to emulate them in the future.

What does Joseph think about all this? It's got to be a headful and dreadful. Up until now he's been fixing cars. His standards have been pretty much black and white. If it works, it's good. If it doesn't work, it's bad. But just "getting the car fixed" is at the lowest level of standards for an auto repair company attempting to become the Most Successful Small Business in the World. There are so many other standards to be pursued, discovered, and established, such as: How clean is the car when it leaves the shop? What other opportunities exist beyond simply the repair the customer needed done? What repairs (call them High Five Fixes™) can the auto repair shop complete, at no cost to the customer whatsoever, that would come as a huge and delightful surprise (call them Delightful Surprises!™)? What, what, what? That's the nature of setting the highest standards. And then, how,

how, how, do you accomplish this when you come face to face with the seeming impossibility of creating them. This is the nature of reaching beyond anything you have ever reached for before. How ungainly Joseph must feel in the face of this miasma of empty spaces. How ungainly *you* must feel! How inadequate it must feel for him and for you, to have to deal with these questions that you have never before asked. What a strange and un-lucid world! At the same time, what an interesting and exciting world it is!

Rule #6: Write the Exquisite Story

Your company's story must be exquisite—deeply felt, surely told. It must be a story that all of your people believe, tell, feel, say, explain, and explore. Your company is not the product of the story; your story is a product of your company. First the company, then the story. Remarkable as it might seem, such stories are the stuff of which legends are made. And your company, the company we are creating here—Joseph's new company, your new company—will become a legend, as will Joseph, as will you, as will everyone who has taken on the mission to invent the Most Successful Small Business in the World. What a story to be told! Imagine, just imagine . . . 10,000 stores! How does a normal human being achieve that? How does he or she even *begin* to achieve that? How does he even *imagine* he can achieve that? What possesses such a human being, when the idea compels him to reach out so far? The story of such a person, of such an endeavor, is a story to behold. It begins as all things begin, with a thought. It begins with the thought which gives birth to this company, to the Most Successful Small Business in the World.

It is a thought unlike any thought that had preceded it. This thought is born out of a series of questions. In this case, the questions "What am I doing here? What is my life all about? Where am I going?" will stimulate a string of thoughts, each of which leads to the next, and that to the very next, all of which create a string of feelings. Each, like a string of mostly beautiful, and some very painful, beads, clings to the other. Each thought clings to another thought, as a lush and lustrous tapestry is woven, stitch by stitch, to complete an original picture. This is a picture you have never seen before. This picture is to the viewer, to you, to Joseph, a promise of more. It's a promise of something never seen before. It's promise of your life rolling out in front of you in the form of a new world. This is the story your company must live to unfold.

Rule # 7: Live Your Story

The story you've told will come to nothing if it is not fully lived. It must be lived by your company, by your people, by you. From the moment your story is first told, it must be documented. Once documented, all of the pieces of the story must be exemplified in action. Every part, every action of your company, the Most Successful Small Business in the World, must live in the story, must take place in the story. Each part, each character, must participate in earnest, not only in the story, but in the life of your company, and in the world. You, as the founder of your company, must live your part in the story, in your company, in your life, as the chief protagonist of your story. This story, however, is nonfiction. It is real—as real as you are. The part you play is real. The company is real. The history that the story re-tells, again and again, is real. All of the ups and downs of it are real. It is all so real, and so dramatic, that at times when you tell the story, you stand in amazement that you have actually done all these things told in the story. This is the story that you will tell about your company. The story that you created, built, nurtured is about the Most Successful Small Business in the World.

You must live your story, because if you don't, it isn't a true story. And if it isn't a true story then your company isn't a true company. And if your company isn't a true company, then the world that you live in isn't a true world. Hear me when I say that. If your company isn't a true company, then the world you live in isn't a true world. If that is the case, then none of what we have said here matters. And if none of what we have said here matters, then nothing matters at all. So, if your story calls for impeccable white starched shirts, wear, above all, impeccable white starched shirts. And if your company calls for an expensive navy blue suit, wear, above all, an expensive navy blue suit. And if your company calls for smiling people, then, above all, surround yourself with delightfully smiling people all, or forever hold your peace. You are your story. Your story is you. You either live it to the fullest, or your world comes falling down like Humpty Dumpty did, and all the King's men too!

IN ALL MARKETS

In this, the Fourth Principle, we are also instructed that the Most Successful Small Business in the World will not only be sustainable in all economic conditions, but "in all markets, providing meaningful, highly differentiated results to all its customers."

This says exactly what you are thinking it says. Your company, once conceived, designed, built, and developed, can live everywhere your chosen customer does, provided that there are enough customers to support an ongoing business (your business). This then begs the question, how many of them (your customers) does it take to support an ongoing business (your business)? And of course when I speak of an "ongoing business," I am speaking of just one of the 10,000. It is simple to say that every company that presumes to grow substantially must ask, and then answer, the very same question. How many customers does it take to support a McDonald's? How many to support a Hilton hotel? How many to support a Citgo service station? How many to support a Fantastic Sams? The answer is always different. *Your* answer will also be different. Your answer will depend on your business model, which will depend on your assumptions, which will depend on the outcome you intend to produce. How many times do you expect your customer to come back, with what frequency, and with what revenue objectives? These answers will determine your trading zone, the geographic market, within which your company attracts regular customer visits on a hopefully regular basis of X. X is the hope your 10,000 stores operate by, succeed by, become the Most Successful Small Business in the World by, with exacting consistency, producing in each and every one of the 10,000 as though pulling a rabbit out of a perfectly shaped hat exactly the X you predicted.

And that is all made possible—the rabbit out of the hat trick—because you have built, with unerring standards, the perfectly replicable model as dictated in the Fourth Principle. This says that your business is a system, with elaborately interchangeable parts that are not so elaborate after all. The parts are intricately, intelligently designed pieces of your world-famous puzzle, whose pieces and parts, and sum total, are broadly and delightedly known throughout the world as nobody else but you!

Poetry is what happens
When nothing else can.

—Charles Bukowski
writing from *The Flash of Lightning*
Behind the Mountain

Chapter 5

The Fifth Principle

A Small Business Is a School in Which Its Employees Are Students, with the Intention, Will, and Determination to Grow

Without continual growth and progress, such words as improvement, achievement, and success have no meaning.
—Benjamin Franklin

How does Joseph handle this? For that matter, how do you? Your new company is a school, where each and every employee is a student, with the intention, will, and determination to grow.

At the heart of this principle is the notion that we are, none of us, complete as we are. For us to be complete, there must be a drive to grow beyond our current understanding, our current capabilities, our current knowledge, skills, and perspective. The fulfillment of completeness is the desire for growth. It is the desire to grow our understanding, our capabilities, our knowledge, and our skill, and with these attributes, our perspective, about ourselves, about the world, about life, about the universe, about where we fit.

That this should happen in a small business seems absurd on the face of it, knowing what we know about the small businesses we have worked in, and the people who own and manage them.

Knowing what we know about Joseph.

Knowing what we know about ourselves.

Knowing how little we know.

So, if this principle is absurd on the face of it, where would we find within this principle the wisdom that calls it forth as an essential ingredient of the Most Successful Small Business in the World?

For this to occur, we must look more deeply into the reality of small business, the reality of learning, and the reality of the people, all people, who go to work every day to make a living. There is no more repetitive, organized reality in the world than that of small business—millions upon millions upon untold millions of them—in every country throughout the world.

More than 90 percent of all employed people work in a small business of some sort, even if they're working alone as sole proprietors. The so-called underground economy is nothing other than a hodgepodge of people working for a living, under the radar, unnoticed by government, or by any of us for that matter. They are unnoticed, but working, creating extra, or not so extra bucks, just to get by. Just to make it through the day. They are invisible people, but determined people. They hustle, hustle, hustle their very lives away.

These people will spend the majority of their lives out there "working for a living," not of course in any particular one small business, but in some small business—perhaps in their own small business, or somebody else's small business. Doing it, doing it, doing it, day after day.

And unless they continue studying while working (as many do, and many more hope to do . . . to get a better job, in yet another small business), their education stops.

In short, most people stop learning once they go to work. There is little to be learned in most small businesses, other than the job one does.

Of course, that does not mean that they have to stop learning. It simply means that in most cases most people already know what they need to know to be employed by a small business; otherwise, they wouldn't be employable.

There is little time, and little funding, available in most small businesses for anything other than what goes on in the business.

Learning, if it goes on at all in a small business, is pragmatic at best. And, worse than that, specifically pragmatic, to what goes on in *this* small business.

Learning, if it goes on at all in a small business, has to do with productivity and performance—how to do your job better in our business to produce better results in our business.

If the new skill or knowledge adds value to the employee's ability to get a job in someone else's small business, that's part of the gamble for the small business owner. But few make the gamble, in any case, to educate an employee.

Unfortunately as well, little of such learning or education of that sort goes on in most small businesses. People are too busy working for a living to give such learning much thought, or to invest much, if any, time and money in employee education and training.

On the other hand, Joseph is not simply running any old business. Old Joseph had already done that as he fixed cars.

No, Joseph—you—are about to go on a journey unlike any journey you have ever gone on before. You are going to create the Most Successful Small Business in the World, with 10,000 outlets, stores, shops.

And to do that, you are going to need some exceptional people. You are going to need people who presumably will have the ability to grow one store, outlet, or shop into 10,000 of them. And you need them to do it like it has never been done before. But, who has that ability?

Who among all of those people working in small businesses out there—or, even in big businesses—possesses the ability to grow one outlet, shop, or store into 10,000 faithful replicates of it?

Who among them possesses the understanding, capabilities, knowledge, skill and perspective to pull it off? Who among them can create the Most Successful Small Business in the World? Who among them can invent the all-time greatest that ever was built?

Where would we even begin to find such people? Well, we wouldn't *find* them. We would need to *create* them.

CREATING THE RIGHT PEOPLE

The Fifth Principle says that you don't *find* the right people, you *create* the right people. And to create the right people means you need to put them through school.

Continuous school.

The never-stop kind of school.

The school of continuous learning.

No school they have ever been to will prepare them for your new company.

No school they have ever been to possessed the knowledge or the interest to prepare their students to become what you, in your new company, expect of them.

Your people must become leaders in a totally new world.
Your people must hunger for something that no one has even thought of before.
Your people must become voracious students. And you, and Joseph, must become voracious teachers. And what you teach must be voraciously designed to meet your otherworldly expectations, the demands of your 10,000 stores.

Step One: Asking the Right Questions

Question One: What do your students—your employees—need to learn, to continuously prepare them for your otherworldly pursuit, your otherworldly expectations?

I think of it as right work. They need to learn what the words "right work" mean. They need to be able to do right work rightly. They need to know when they see right work. They need to know what the experience of doing right work feels like. They need to know what the result of right work looks like; what it produces.

The theory of right work is a course you need to teach in your school. It is a fundamental course, a baseline course, a course that serves all of the courses that stem from it. The theory of right work is the course that every new employee will be required to take . . . even before they become new employees.

It is the philosophical bedrock of your 10,000 stores. It's what makes them so special. It's what makes them an integral part of the Most Successful Small Business in the World.

It is a philosophical dialectic, a conversation that you, as teacher, will have with each and every new prospective employee to induct them into the 10,000 store lexicon, the life language that defines your 10,000 store logic, the conceptual understanding of how one small business can become the logos for 9,999 more. The 9,999 more theory of everything is encapsulated within the theory of right work, as it describes what must occur within the first store, for it to become the perfect DNA for the 9,999 more. It is the school through which an uncommon language of business is spoken by all who study there, by all who practice what they study there, and by all who believe in the theory of right work. Your employees believe in it so much that they aspire to become masters of the theory of right work to teach it wherever they go, to whomever they meet.

This of course is at the heart of the story of the 10,000 stores.

This is something we have spoken about so many times before.

You must learn the theory of right work, which means you must first learn what that theory is. You must invent that theory, even now, as I am sharing the idea of that theory with you here. You must begin to design that theory-in-practice even as we are pursuing the question itself right here, together.

And you will only be able to answer this question, by asking another question, which is, "What is wrong work?" If there is a right work, then of course there is a wrong work.

Until you understand the devastatingly negative impact of wrong work, you will never be able to appreciate the remarkably enlightening nature of right work.

To the degree that appreciation doesn't rise full circle within Joseph, within you, dear reader, you will never truly understand why this course, the theory of right work is so essential to the soul of your 10,000 stores.

I am reminded of the experience I have had the few times I've elected to go to In-N-Out Burgers in California. The stores are packed with people, always. The stores sell the most ordinary of ordinary food, that is, burgers, fries, soft drinks, and that's it. Remember? Ordinary. Nothing special, as the Zen master said, but oh something special.

Their people, the people who are dressed in their In-N-Out dress code of white and yellow and red—impeccably dressed I might add—even as they perform all of the absolutely ordinary functions of cutting fries, cooking burgers, heating buns, taking orders, serving orders, and cleaning the premises, just like all of this is being done in millions of restaurants throughout the world. But, and here's the point—they're doing it *not* just like it's being done in millions of restaurants throughout the world. They are doing it *only* as "In-N-Out" does it.

See the people. They're bright. They're eager. They're awake. They're originals.

They look fresh, as if this day is their very first day. They look like they just got out of school. They look like they were just issued their brand, spanking-new uniform. They look like they're proud to wear it. They look like they're hot to trot and to give you their unique experience. They look like they're In-N-Out babies, on the In-N-Out path, a path that is going somewhere. Somewhere important. Somewhere each and every one of them know. We don't know. But we get it. And that's why their places are packed.

"The food," someone says, "it's the food, Gerber."

But, I tell you, it is not the food. It's the school. It's what they've learned there at In-N-Out University. It's what they continue to learn there, and in their store. It's what inspires them to reach further. It's all about the theory of right work and nothing else.

In the course called the theory of right work, we will learn such subjects as:

- **Presence (101):** In this class, we will discover what it means to be present, called by some, the un-theoretical reality of where you are.

- **Taking Action (101):** In this class, we will discover the difference between taking action from the inside, and being moved into action from the outside.

- **The Nature of Results (101):** In this class, we will discuss the different kind of results: passive results; active results; intentional results; accidental results. And if it is an accidental result can it rightly be called a result? And, if so, what would it be called? And so forth, and so on.

- **On the Subject of Time** (101): In this class, we will discover the many different kinds of Time we are confronted with in our lives, at home, and on the job: quick time; slow time; moving time; stopped time; just in time; out of time; no time; and many, many more. Time is not what you make it. Time is what makes you. Your relationship with time, defines your actions within time. Your relationship with your actions, defines the quality of time you assign to it. And then, of course, there is the world of eternity. Which raises an entirely different level of conversation. But, that's another course. We'll get to *that* course in good time.

- And many, many more.

Have I lost my mind?

Am I just playing with you?

No, absolutely not. Trust me in this. I am not playing with you. Every word so far has defined my 10,000 school mind. What it says is that in my creation of New, I have lost my sense of old. I have lost my sense of boredom. I have lost my sense of nothing original going on. I have lost my sense of what it means to be stuck in the dull old world. I have lost my sense of what it means to be dying in a dull old business. I am leaving behind the world of not seeing, the world of not creating, the world of just fixing cars.

A business client once told me, with a passion he hadn't felt in years, that I had pushed him out of his sleep. He called it his "sleep," as though it was actually a place he had been confined to. When he spoke of it, I could feel what he meant. He meant that he had stopped living. He had literally stopped *living*. Of course he was doing all the things he had programmed himself to do. He was programmed to "do." But there was no life in just doing. He wasn't present most of the time. He was simply going through the motions.

The theory of right work is all about being awake; being alive; asking questions about subjects no one has ever discussed with us before. It's about asking questions in a way no one has ever asked us before. The questions are asked for a reason that no one has even taken seriously before, because they thought they were already awake. In their state of sleep, they didn't know they were asleep. They thought this activity they went through each day was what life was meant to be; it is what they were relinquished to do. And they thought that, because no one had ever raised the question with them before. In the 10,000 store school, these questions, and many, many more will be asked, will be raised, will be challenged, and every student will be challenged to ask. They will not be asked theoretically, but rather they will be asked actually, truly, rightly, in the only way that an awake person would be expected to raise these questions. They will be challenged to become fully awake.

What are these questions? I ask you again. I ask you, I ask Joseph, I ask you, dear reader. I ask you to ask yourself, "What are these questions?" and to ask that question again and again. Let me suggest just a few.

A List of Some of the Right Questions

- How many ways are there to tell time?

- How will one know when she or he is doing the right work?

- How can one be asleep and awake at the same time?

- What is an expectation, and how do expectations affect outcomes?

- How is it possible to know the truth?

- How can events be determined to be true, untrue, or one's impression of the truth?

- What does the word "relative" mean?

- What does the word "absolute" mean?

- What does the word "objective" mean?

- What does the word "subjective" mean?

- Is it more important to be "objective" or "subjective"?

- Is history real?

- How can we know the truth, or falsehood, of history?

- If we can't know the difference between the truth of history or the falsehood of history, how can we determine what to do today?

- What does the word "meaning" mean?

- Can a company mean something?

- Can a human being mean something?

- Does life have meaning?

- If life has meaning, what does it mean, and how can one determine what it means?

- Is government necessary?

- If government is necessary, what are its most important ingredients?

- If government isn't necessary, how would decisions be made without it?

- Could human beings live a life without government?

- If so, how would that society be organized?

- Is there a process through which people make decisions?

- If there is a decision-making process, how does it work?

- If there isn't a decision-making process, how are decisions made?

- Are there right decisions and wrong decisions?

- How would one know the difference between the two?

- How do people think?

- What is the process through which people think?

- Is there a difference between a "conclusion" and a "decision"?

- Is there a difference between an opinion and a fact?

- How would one know the difference?

- How would one know the difference if the opinion or fact is an emphatic statement made by another person?

- How would one know the difference if the opinion or fact is a statement made by you?

- What does the word "true" mean?

- What does the word "false" mean?

- Do people really tell the truth?

- Do people tell falsehoods intentionally?

- Is it possible to tell a falsehood and not know it?

- Is it possible to believe something to be true even when that something is false?

- Can a business have meaning?

- Can the people working in a business have meaning?

- Can the meaning of a product be determined objectively?

- Can one product mean more than another product?

- Is the term "better" capable of being judged morally?

- Is there a moral reality to doing business?

- Can the functions in a business be conducted morally?

- What is the difference between a moral choice and an ethical choice?

- Which choice would one prefer to make—a moral choice or an ethical choice?

- How many words does the average high school graduate use effectively?

- Is the use of words a moral reality, an ethical reality, or a simple measure of intelligence?

- Does the standard measure of intelligence really matter in your world? In our world? In their world?

- Is there something more important than intelligence?

- What about Gardner's eight multiple intelligences?

- What are the eight multiple intelligences?

- Is it important to have strength in one or more of Gardner's intelligences than the traditional intelligences? Which intelligences would I want, or need, in my employees?

- How do I determine what intelligences potential and current employees possess?

- Can these intelligences be developed, or are they inborn?

- What does emotional intelligence really mean?

- Is emotional intelligence more important in running your business, and in conducting your life, than intelligence or intellect?

- What is a story?

- What is a myth?

- What is the reason for asking all these damned questions?

- What does the word "reason" mean?

ALL THIS IN THE CONTEXT OF 10,000 STORES

And of course, it is in the context of school. It's in the context of the school for 10,000 stores. Remember why we're doing this. We're doing this to grow our people.

From the very first moment they have heard our story and said a profound Yes! to the wish to become a employee in your store. They wish to be a character in your wonderful story.

And, of course, they have also said, Yes! to becoming a student in our school for 10,000 stores.

And, of course they have said, Yes! to learning to grow, to truly grow to a level they never thought possible, as professionals and as thoughtful human beings.

So they can become masters, one and all, of all of the subjects they will learn in our school for 10,000 stores.

They have never heard of a school like ours. Never.

No one, they tell us, has ever cared to teach them the lessons they hope to learn in our school:

Lessons about life and lessons about work.

Lessons about money and lessons about management.

And most of all, lessons about entrepreneurship:

How to create a business of their own.

How to develop the skills of independence, and marketing, management, and entrepreneurship.

How to think—especially how to think.

How to think originally.

How to think and act like a leader.

How to develop beyond where they are or ever have been, to become expert growers, expert knowers, expert of all of the functions that have made 10,000 stores possible.

They wish to embrace and internalize all of the things that have made it possible for us to create the Most Successful Small Business in the World.

SO WHAT WILL THEY LEARN IN OUR SCHOOL?

They will learn the general lessons and they will learn the specific application of the general lessons in our business of 10,000 stores.

They will learn, as we've already said, how to think.

They will learn how to think about relationships, about systems, and about systems of relationships.

They will learn how each part of our company relates to each and every other part of our company, and why that is important.

They will learn about what we define in 10,000 stores as the "systems matrix."

They will learn how and why the systems matrix is not many things, but one thing.

The one thing that we can depend on in 10,000 stores is the continual creation of the ethos, the logic, and the performance of 10,000 stores in each and every store, in each and every person in each and every store, in each and every transaction in each and every store, in each and every relationship within each and every store.

They will learn how all this is reflected in the simple and not so simple tasks in each and every store, exactly as it is done in each and every store. They will learn the 10,000 store way. They will learn, just as they learn in McDonald's the McDonald's way; in In-N-Out, the In-N-Out way; in Starbucks, the Starbucks way. Each system of stores—of shops, of service centers, of nurseries, of offices—possesses its own way in accordance with the best way model, the business design model, the entrepreneurial model. Without these unique models, none of the above businesses would possess the energy, imagination, or color to accede to the highest. They would simply be raw commodities—simply a hamburger restaurant, a coffee shop, an auto repair shop.

In the Most Successful Small Business in the World, it matters exactly how the hamburger is wrapped and what it is wrapped in. It matters exactly how and when the floors are cleaned and what they look like when they are done. It matters exactly what colors are used and how they are designed to complement each other, and how color affects the customer. It matters exactly how the counter person greets the customer and what he or she says.

Everything in our 10,000 stores matters, exactly. Without mattering exactly, it would not be the 10,000 stores. It could not be. And all of that must be taught and learned and mastered.

If there is no school, there is no rabbit in the hat. And if there is no rabbit in the hat, there will be nothing special to teach to our people. And if there is nothing special to teach to our people, there will be nothing special for them to do. And if there is nothing special for them to do, how will we win our customers' hearts and minds?

Therefore, it is obvious that in our school, our people will learn about the rabbit in the hat, and come to love that story. They will come to know how to pull the rabbit out of the hat. They will learn to do this flawlessly, gracefully.

On a more prosaic level, they will learn about innovation, quantification, and orchestration. They will learn why and how orchestration is the secret sauce behind our most emphatic claim to being the Most Successful Small Business in the World. They will come to understand that orchestration means integrity, and integrity means the right stuff, and the right stuff means we are doing the right work rightly, and that we are doing it every single time.

They will come to love our ability to perform, which is their ability to perform. And they will come to learn exactly how to do that. They will come to do that with every small task and every large task. In McDonald's Hamburger U, the student learns the magic underlying the minute. In our 10,000 stores, they will learn how every bolt and every nut and every ingredient of every process serves to produce the magic minute. Every piece, every process, in a complexity of simplicity, unites to become the remarkably original thing that the 10,000 stores represent to everyone who is captured by our message and the meaning underlying our message.

They will come to appreciate how rare it is in the world of business-as-usual to perform exactly, because the world of business-as-usual has few standards against which it performs.

A standard-less world cannot be compared to the unlikely world 10,000 stores has created for itself. We will live by our own measures. And our own measures are the only relevant measures, because *we* didn't make them up, our customers did.

Our customers made them up by their frustrations, their disappointments, their challenges, and unrealized desires. Our customers made them up and then told us about them. And they told us about them simply because we asked. We asked, we asked, and we asked.

And our competitors didn't. Our competitors assumed; they never asked. And even if they had asked, our competitors wouldn't have listened. They didn't have the time. They didn't have the education. They didn't have the desire. We at our school of 10,000 stores are on fire with our desire.

That's what it means to be a great student . . . to be on fire with our desire. That is, above all, what we teach in our school.

The school of 10,000 stores.

we are hardly ever
as strong
as that which we
create.

—Charles Bukowski
The Curse
Slouching toward Nirvana

Chapter 6

The Sixth Principle

A Small Business Must Manifest the Higher Purpose upon Which It Was Seeded, the Vision It Was Meant to Exemplify, the Mission It Was Intended to Fulfill

Every man must decide whether he will walk in the light of creative altruism or in the darkness of destructive selfishness.
—Martin Luther King, Jr.

Higher purpose is a strange and dangerous thing. A therapist friend of mine once looked at me skeptically when I said the words "higher purpose" as though I was expounding upon something that lived outside the ken of a normal human being. (To my therapist friend, I discovered, *all* human beings are "normal human beings.")

That higher purpose was, to my therapist friend, simply a psychological phenomenon, as I imagine, in my therapist friend's mind, all such ideas are. I tried to describe to him what I meant and found it more difficult than what I imagined it would be when I started out. "I mean that there are more important issues and less important issues," I said.

"A more important issue might be the question, what is it that makes us consumers?

"A less important issue might be the answer, that we buy things.

"A more important issue might be the desire to live a moral life.

"A less important issue might be the desire to produce $100,000 a year.

"A more important issue might be a conversation like the one we're having.

"A less important issue might be a conversation about football.

"A more important question might be the meaning of marriage, why we commit to it, and what does it mean to marry, in relationship to living a meaningful life.

"A less important issue might be the conflict between husbands and wives."

"More important to whom?" my therapist friend asked.

"To one guy," he said, "football is the most important subject on the planet. To another guy, he couldn't care less. In other words, the word 'higher' has no relevance other than how it relates to the person you're speaking about. It's all personal.

"It's all relative to the individual and what's gone on in his life and what's going on in his life now."

"Yes," I answered, "but the word 'higher' as I'm using it pertains to one's values.

"If football sits at the top of the hierarchy for the guy you're talking about, I would hate to see what sits at the bottom of it.

"In other words, if football is what attracts his highest attention, then his life is fairly bleak."

"Why do you say that?" asked my therapist friend.

I had the most uncomfortable thought that I wasn't going to get any further with this conversation. My therapist friend seemed trapped in an old habit and not really open to the essence of what I was saying to him. But, I couldn't help myself. I had to understand what I was thinking, what was moving my need to get him to see what was important in this.

"Mother Theresa lived what I would think of as a higher-purpose life. Muhammad Yunus lives what I would think of as a higher purpose life. Each of them, in their own way, has engaged the world to alleviate pain and suffering, with love and attention and determination. I will guarantee you that neither of them had ever had a conversation about football. Or about the television show they watched the night before. It's not that they didn't possess lower instincts and needs. We all have. I'm sure they did, and, in Mr. Yunus's case, still does. It's just that their lower lives didn't influence the life they lived. I think that's possible for all of us. And I think, if it is possible for all of us, then all of us are paying a huge price for not pursuing the question."

■　　■　　■

My therapist friend and I never did resolve the issue. He sees people as they are; I see people as they could be. But, it's not that I don't see people as they are. I do. I deal with this every day, both in myself, and in others. If I didn't, I could never communicate with them, I could never understand them, I could never move them to see anything other than what they believe themselves to be. But, I also see the huge difference between those with no higher aim and those whose lives are driven by it, which is what I see as the distinction between the entrepreneur of the past and the new entrepreneur.

The entrepreneur of the past is consumed by people as they are, exploits them as they are, panders to them as they are, excites them as they are, terrifies them as they are. Read any advertisement you choose to, and you will see what I mean. "You deserve a break today." And the consumer says, "You bet I do." "Just do it!" And the consumer says, "I will!" We don't like to think we are so easily manipulated, but of course we are. All of consumerism is built on the old entrepreneur's model of fear and desire. Ninety-nine percent of all companies today (my statistic, nobody else's) are built on the old entrepreneur's model of becoming a master of manipulating people as they are. The more you know about how people are, the more successfully you can manipulate them. The foundation for the "new science" of NLP (neurolinguistic programming) is built on knowing more about the tics and tocks of people than has ever been known before. Knowing, so as to increase your effectiveness at communicating with them, at convincing them, at knowing what works and what doesn't—all to get what you want. Pavlov's dogs were no better and no different. If this, then that. Ring the bell, give the food, food, bell, the two become one. Neither the consumer, nor Pavlov's dogs, are any wiser.

Is that what we are truly interested in doing? Well, of course, if we want to produce a result. But perhaps there's a better result than to simply stimulate the consumer to buy a product or service.

Perhaps there's a higher aim, something more worthy of our time. That's the role of the new entrepreneur, in this age of the new entrepreneur. That higher aim is not to stimulate a purchase. Rather it is to provide a result that authentically serves a human being in the process of emerging from where they are to where they could be. Once the authenticity of the result is seen, understood, valued by the customer—as essential to their life—the sale has been already achieved.

But, for that to happen, the result that's promised must be achievable. It is no longer acceptable to the new entrepreneur to stimulate a sale, the result of which is that the vast majority of those who purchase the product or service end up in exactly the same place they were when the sale was made.

I saw an infomercial by a "billionaire" who has created a course through which his students can become "billionaires" too. Just like him. Is that true? Are his students truly going to become "billionaires"? Of course not. Not one of them will. But, as far as our "billionaire" is concerned, he taught them what they needed to know and what to do to make the transformation occur. Too bad if they didn't do it. Too bad if they weren't as determined, smart, clever, persistent, or outrageous as their master was and certainly is. The course he is selling costs about $120,000 a year! Can you imagine somebody believing that, buying that, hoping for that—that they too will become a billionaire? What possesses a person to believe such a ridiculous tale? What possesses a person to pay someone to produce the impossible? What makes it possible for our "billionaire" to pull such a rabbit out of a hat, without anyone catching on to the fact that there is no rabbit, and there is no hat, is just the manipulation of the levers that manipulate the undiscerning mind, the mind as we are, the mind that hopes for the impossible, the mind that is unwilling to see that the emperor indeed is wearing no clothes, despite the fact that he has convinced you he is.

Look instead at Muhammad Yunus and his Grameen Bank. Look at the millions of impoverished women he made a promise to, the promise of self-sufficiency, the promise that he has kept millions upon millions of times.

What does that self-sufficiency look like? What does that self-sufficiency mean?

It means they can produce food for their table. It means they can provide education for their children. It means that they can put a roof—a real roof, not a makeshift roof—over their family's heads. It means they can live with dignity. It means that they, with merely the fundamental skills they already possess, without going into elaborate training, elaborate transformation, can produce an income stream beyond anything they had ever imagined before.

What occurs when a woman accustomed to a life of impoverishment, on so many levels, discovers that with one simple change in her environment—the change provided by Grameen Bank—she suddenly possesses the ability to fulfill her and her family's essential needs? What happens is she begins to *grow*. She begins to see more than she has ever seen before. She begins to feel the dignity that had never been hers. Never. She begins to feel—for the very first time in her life—like a growing, capable human being.

How extraordinary Muhammad Yunus must feel!

How extraordinary you will feel as you begin to pursue this dream, this vision, this purpose, this mission—just as he did!—with the invention and creation of your Most Successful Small Business in the World.

THE FIVE COMPONENTS OF A HIGHER PURPOSE

In my two books, *E-Myth Mastery* and *The E-Myth Enterprise*, I described the five essential functions of a world-class company: inspiration, education, training, coaching, and mentoring.

The product of inspiration is an epiphany, a moment of seeing.

The product of education is understanding.

The product of training is application.

The product of coaching is implementation.

The product of mentoring is continuous improvement.

These functions, or organizational skills, might best be thought of as core competencies.

Additionally in *E-Myth Mastery* and *The E-Myth Enterprise*, I described the five essential skills of an entrepreneur. These skills are concentration, discrimination, organization, innovation, and communication.

The product of *concentration* is the ability to focus your attention.

The product of *discrimination* is the ability to choose where to focus your attention.

The product or *organization* is to create order out of chaos.

The product of *innovation* is to continually discover, and implement, a better way of doing what you do.

The product of *communication* is to expand your reach.

In *The E-Myth Revisited,* I described the seven steps of the business development process: your primary aim, your strategic objective, your organizational strategy, your management strategy, your people strategy, your marketing strategy, and your systems strategy.

In *Awakening the Entrepreneur Within,* I detailed the four essential personalities of an entrepreneur: the dreamer, the thinker, the storyteller, and the leader. The dreamer has a dream. The thinker has a vision. The storyteller has a purpose. The leader has a mission.

When we speak of the five components of a higher purpose, we're organizing the five essential functions. The five essential skills, the seven steps of the business development process, and the dream, vision, purpose, and mission of the entrepreneur into a model that builds itself, as a ladder, to reach for the higher purpose.

The steps in that ladder are what I call the five components of a higher purpose.

The first step is *awakening.*

The second step is *discovering.*

The third step is *experiencing.*

The fourth step is *internalizing.*

The fifth step is *becoming.*

Let's take a look at each of those steps, one step at a time.

THE FIRST STEP: AWAKENING

We are sound asleep. We are lost in the associations that confuse our mind. We do not *know* that we are asleep. We have been taught that the sleep we are in, is in fact awake. We think that we are making conscious decisions. We think that we are acting through the deliberate conscious choices we seem to be making. But, that is not true. Our choices are not conscious, they are unconscious. Our choices are reactions created by associations that we have accumulated automatically, mechanically, all the time creating in us the illusion that we have done these things with intelligence, with thought, with a consideration of all the elements that make up this pattern we call our life. According to a man named Gurdjieff, and his primary voice, Mr. Ouspenski, in his extraordinary book, *In Search of the Miraculous*, we are anything but conscious human beings. We are machines. Automatons. Robots. We are asleep.

Awakening occurs in the moment when we see ourselves for what we are. We see how enslaved we are to our feelings, our reactions, our stream of uncreated, autonomous thoughts. We experience ourselves as Gurdjieff described us, or as the film *The Matrix* described us so well . . . as machines. We are caught up in a web of intricate interactions that come about without our true participation, without our true understanding, without our knowledge of the intricate pattern of the whole. What happens when we awaken, when we "remember our self" as Gurdjieff called us to do? We have this sudden seeing, this moment of profound clarity, this deeply felt desire to awaken even more. To become the "I" that we all believed we were, the "I am" in truth. We become something other than the product of everything that goes on about us that we can't even begin to explain. We become the center of ourselves. We become the *mover* as opposed to the *moved*.

As I write this, I think back to what I said, disparagingly, about the billionaire, who invited all of us to become billion-aires too. Am I doing the same thing here? Am I inviting you to become something you will never become? Am I stimulating your greed, your hunger for more, simply for the sake of writing this book? Am I creating an expectation that is impossible for most to fulfill? Am I offering you the same result that the billionaire is offering, knowing even as I do so, that you won't even take step one? Or, if you do, that you won't take step two?

Am I asleep, too?

No, I am not "scamming" you. I am completely serious, and I believe and know that you can do this. Yes, *you*! But am I asleep?

THE SECOND STEP: DISCOVERING

Yes, of course I am asleep. Sometimes. I come in and out of it. It happens to me, as it does to everyone. I am in constant reaction to influences and actions that occur in the world around me, and I am moved by them to feel this, to think that. I sometimes have little or no control over the "this" that I feel, or the "that" which rises up in me. And I see that. Who else sees that? Who else can see that? The one who is awakened can see that. The Michael that is awakened, somehow, to the instantaneous reality of my sleep, my reactivity, can see that. The feelings and thoughts that arise in me of their own power, without any truly deliberate conscious participation on my part, can see that. And the moment that I see that, I come to realize that, feel that, there is the discovery that transcends that — the discovery by me. The discovery *of* me. The one who has been awakened. The one who has been called to see. The one who has been asleep. And so, discovery is a critical step in the awakened and awakening state, which is continually being awakened by becoming aware of what

I see, and who it is that sees it. Not conscious yet, no. But awake, at least.

THE THIRD STEP: EXPERIENCING

As discovering occurs, I begin to taste a new dimension of experiencing. I am actually experiencing not my association of, but my sensation of, the direct experience of impressions that I am having awakening in me. These impressions speak to me more fully, more dimensionally so to speak, with greater authenticity, with greater intensity, than I have ever experienced before. I stood before a person in one of those remarkable states once, and remember, even now, some 35 years later, exactly what that experience felt like to me. I knew, in that exact moment, that I was there, that she was there, that *we* were there, and I knew who we were, standing there, experiencing that moment to a degree none of the moments that preceded it had ever been experienced. It was astonishing—the color, the shape, the energy that possessed us in that moment. Doing nothing remarkable, simply being there. You can remember moments like that as well. Not dramatic moments, not stunningly remarkable experiences, but experiences of being present to a degree you had rarely ever experienced before that. And that experience just came to you. You couldn't explain where it came from or why. Nor could you repeat that experience, could you? No, extraordinary experiences came on their own, and left on their own. Imagine what your life would be like if you could *create* such experiences. Imagine if those experiences were replicable. Imagine who you would be. Well, I know that we can create such experiencing. I know that it is possible. I know that it is possible for each of us to do that, to experience that, to come into our own.

THE FOURTH STEP: INTERNALIZING

If experiencing can be heightened to a dimension rarely felt, then the next step to occur is internalizing those experiences, and the impact they have on us, to raise our level of being to another level. As we take these steps, from awakening, to discovering, to experiencing, to internalizing, we begin to transform into another being. This is the life of living. The Lubavitcher Rebbe, Rabbi Menachem M. Schneerson, once said, "Run! And if you cannot run—Walk! And if you cannot walk—Crawl! But, always advance, advance, advance!" As our higher, more vibrant experiences appear to us, as we begin to internalize their force within us, as we move through a new dimension of our life and the living of our life, we are coming into relationship with the "I" who is our true center, our soul, or *neshama*, within our life, as well as the soul of the life living continuously around us. How do I know that? I know that, because I have experienced that. How do I know what these experiences mean? I know, because I have come into relationship with my life, and have internalized it into my continuously moving state of being. I am 73, as I write this to you. Even now, I am creating a new life. I am moving beyond where I have been, and discovering new possibilities through the experience of new realities, through the internalization of this new state of being. And yet, I know I am still asleep. Awakening, yes, but still asleep. I experience my sleep through the astonishing realization when I am awake and awakening. I experience my sleep, and internalize those experiences as I discover a new being in me, one who has tried to become more than I am, but has not succeeded as often as I would have wished myself to. I am 73, and yet the process is continually moving. This can be true of you as well. But, only as you awaken, discover, experience, and internalize on an ongoing basis, pushing the momentum forward to run, or to walk, or to crawl, as the great Rebbe Menachem Schneerson said, but always moving forward.

THE FIFTH STEP: BECOMING

As we internalize these new impressions, the experiences which flood our perceptions with new found life—color, forms, energy, meaning—translate themselves into becoming, the movement forward, the continually ascending hierarchy of being. Becoming is a process. Being is a state. The state of being moves forward in the process of becoming successively, beyond the state it had reached one step before. There is no end to this. There is no arriving, other than that which we come upon and then leave. Arriving is always transformed into either entropy or ascending. Entropy is a falling back, a dying. Ascending is a rising toward, an enlivening. The thing we are rising toward is imagined, not real, but lives in the expectation and or hope that there is something more in us, something higher within us, that we are reaching toward. The reality is somewhat other than that. The reality is he who is rising toward, when he is actually rising, that is. Most often we're not. We have either begun to die, or have gone to sleep. We go to sleep upon arriving or even before then. We go to sleep wherever we are, holding on as we do to what we believe we have achieved, lest we lose it.

We are constantly in the fear of losing what we have, when in fact, we have nothing that is our own. Then "Who moves?" you might ask. Who is it in me that moves forward? Who is it in me who is becoming? What am I becoming, if there is nothing toward which my becoming arrives? Is this a process which has no end to it? Is this, as I have said, a figment of our sleeping imagination? Is this a color that resides only somewhere between white and black, but has no presence, no chromatic scale all of its own?

These are all questions you might ask, as you and I move toward our subsequent stage of arriving, and the one after that, and the one after that. But, still, even if there is no place where we will ultimately arrive, there is someplace we have left behind. And in the instant of leaving that which was static, we suddenly experience the movement of our lives. It is all movement. It is all rising. Or it is all ceasing to arrive. Here we are becoming. There too. Here we are becoming our lives.

It is that which possesses the higher meaning, the higher purpose, to which your Most Successful Small Business in the World commits itself. This is the state of moving beyond. This is our purpose, yours and mine.

Miracles are to come. With you I leave a rememberance of miracles: they are somebody who can love and who shall be continually reborn, a human being; somebody who said to those near him, when his fingers would not hold a brush "tie it into my hand"—nothing proving or sick or partial. Nothing false, nothing difficult or easy or small or colossal. Nothing ordinary or extraordinary, nothing emptied or filled, real or unreal; nothing feeble and known or clumsy and guessed. Everywhere tints childrening, innocent spontaneous, true. No—where possibly what flesh and impossibly such a garden, but actually flowers which breasts are among the very mouths of light. Nothing believed or doubted; brain over heart, surface: nowhere hating or to fear; shadow, mind without soul. Only how measureless cool flames of making; only each other building always distinct selves of mutual entirely opening; only alive. Never the murdered finalities of wherewhen and yesno, impotent nongames of wrongright and rightwrong; never to gain or pause, never to rest and never to have: only to grow. Always the beautiful answer who asks a more beautiful question.

—e. e. cummings
Complete Poems 1904–1962

Chapter 7

The Seventh Principle

A Small Business Is the Fruit of a Higher Aim in the Mind of the Person Who Conceived It

What we have done for ourselves alone dies with us; what we have done for others and the world remains and is immortal.
—Albert Pike

So, yes, what I am communicating to you now, this is the higher aim. Not that the principles which preceded this principle were less important than this; they were not. But that is not the point. The point is simply that we have been preparing for this principle, the Seventh Principle all our lives, you and I. Yet, if sleep is our true condition, then we have been asleep to this too. We have ignored the sure voices that have spoken to us over the years of important things. We have allowed ourselves to become mute, deaf, slow, unfeeling, and insensitive to the divine nature of our unsleeping side. We have been, and suffered from, the severe gravity that weights down our earth-bound side. The animal that pants and plods and suffers the heat of our blood, the pulse of our passion, the stodgy stuff of our wanting. That animal passion is not the divine passion. That animal passion harbors no secrets other than the ones that pull us down. This is not the passion that ascends. This is the passion that pulls the ascendant self down. And so it is, with what you and I create.

If we create from the animal side, we create something bound to lower passion. When we create from the divine side, we create something that is born to ascend.

A business can be either, as you and I can be either and/or both.

A business can, for a time, serve the lower or the higher. But if you are to create the Most Successful Small Business in the World, we must create it from the divine side. This is the moment where we choose it.

What would it mean should you do what Muhammad Yunus has done? What would it mean to choose the higher rather than the lower? What would it call for, from you, to actively pursue the needs of your most important customer . . . to raise them up rather than to tie them down?

Think of the products or services you could sell to do either.

What would the products be that tie them down? Cigarettes, alcohol, drugs, pornography, and on and on and on.

What would the products be that raise them up? Education, training, inspiration, meditation, yoga, debt reduction, credit repair, and on and on and on.

Of course, if the latter were designed to sustain their present mind-set, they would do nothing other than that. They wouldn't truly serve the higher need, the movement away from their ordinary life.

So, there must be something added to the product, the service, something that teaches something, other than what it was intended to teach.

It must teach a new lesson, not just an old skill.

A new lesson would be why this particular education, this particular training, this particular service is so important to them.

It would add a tract on values.

It would add a conversation about leading a meaningful life.

It would teach something beyond the practical application of the skills it is teaching, something which provides a foundation for learning, something which creates a question in the student, rather than simply providing a pragmatic answer.

This is the something they left out of school when you were a student.

But, understand too, that if you simply lecture (as you might feel I am doing right now), you will leave them all behind. You will have taught them something, all right, but not the something you could, would, should, have taught—not the something that matters.

In Muhammad Yunus's case, he has taught them about money and how to use it, but he has also taught them something about community. He taught them how people can serve each other, how to sustain each individual's integrity within the community as they do that. He taught them about how to use money to serve a higher purpose, and their reason for being here. He taught them their role as a mother, sister, daughter, wife— their role as a responsible, dignified, human being.

But he didn't teach this with heavy language. Nor with a stick. Nor with a carrot or an indulgence. He didn't teach this by pandering to the women he serves, but instead, by truly serving them, meeting them where they are, with the very same dignity he is teaching them, with the very same authenticity that the community resolves itself to express, to model.

That is what I mean when I speak of a higher aim. That is what I believe must drive the age of the new entrepreneur. It must be driven by a wish to create and to serve with meaning in the deepest sense of that word. Meaning as it is best exemplified by extraordinary works, invented by extraordinary minds, invested in by extraordinarily awake human beings.

AND NOW WE'RE BACK TO JOSEPH

I'm sure you have thought about him. We left him back there in the discussion about 10,000 stores in our conversation about the First Principle and haven't discussed him again.

The Joseph in each of us doesn't want much at all. We just want a place to work, a place to provide us with the freedom we crave, the freedom from someone else's control. We just want a business of our own. As we've also seen throughout this book, the kind of freedom the Joseph in you craves is unfortunately most often an illusion; it doesn't truly exist.

The kind of freedom that Joseph craves stifles us, inhibits us, and controls us even worse than when we are working for someone else. It creates a demand upon us to create the income that a job at least assures us. It adds another worry: a payroll that the boss had to worry about, not you.

But now you're the boss. And the freedom that we all believe a small business of our own creates does not happen on its own. Like all freedom, it depends on you. It requires you to change your behavior from that of an employee to that of an entrepreneur. The entrepreneur is psychologically far afield from the employee in you. He doesn't *want* freedom because he already *has* it. He doesn't create a small business to be free; he creates a small business to express the freedom he already possesses. The entrepreneur is a free soul in a seemingly un-free world. Not that the world is truly un-free; the entrepreneur never thinks of it that way. But the world in which most of us live behaves through controls, because without those controls it can't do what it needs to do. It needs to set the rules that we live by, until we elect to create our own world. The world Joseph lives in—the Joseph in you—controls what Joseph can do or can't do, but only because it needs to.

The problem in Joseph is that he resents the controls but is unwilling to question what role his behavior plays in them. The controls are there because Joseph hasn't evolved to the point where he understands them, the reason for them, and the importance of them. As a result, Joseph rebels, taking his need to be in control of himself and creating a job for himself where he believes there is no longer any need for controls. That's what becoming his own boss means to Joseph. No controls. Or, even worse, that Joseph, now on his own, is free of controls. Joseph has failed to understand that the controls that inhibited him in the job that he had, had nothing to do with him. When he leaves that job, when he goes out on his own, he fails to put in place the controls that are absolutely essential in a business of his own. And because he fails to put in place the controls his business needs, it most often runs out of control. And so does Joseph.

Which also raises the question, What is the meaning of work?

Which brings Joseph back to the original questions, Who am I? Why am I here?

This is essential if Joseph is to generate sufficient energy to pursue the question of a higher aim, to pursue the deeper meaning of his life, to pursue the creation of the Most Successful Small Business in the World, and to pursue the development of a company that is designed to transform the world. That is, if you and I are to achieve this.

In short, if the higher aim is to be realized at all, it must arise in Joseph. It must drive Joseph. It must become Joseph's obsession. It must awaken and intensify Joseph's dissatisfaction with himself, with his willingness to persist as he is, doing what he does, in the way that he does it. This dissatisfaction must be more than just a restive state. It must become Joseph's voice. It must speak from him, and to him, whether he knows how to speak so or not, whether or not he knows from where the voice comes. Until that's the case—until Joseph grows to know, understand, and deeply hear his voice—Joseph must simply make room for the voice, for the passionate sound of it as the voice tells him things he has never heard before. In the beginning, Joseph's voice will be uncertain. In the beginning, your voice will be uncertain. At the outset of discovering your higher aim, you will not trust it, nor will you trust yourself. You will feel like a stranger in a strange land. But, as we are pursuing this, the Seventh Principle, we are, in the main, pursuing our self, that center of our being. We are pursing that one, the elected one, the one who has been given a destiny. We are seeking the one, within ourselves, with the destiny to create a new world.

Do you realize that yet? Do you realize that you, the one reading this sentence right now, have been given a destiny to create a new world? You were given that even before you were born. You were given that when your soul entered your mother's body, when the physical and the spiritual made that connection, that electrical spark, that commitment to come to earth, that divine inspiration which culminated in your birth. Do you realize that yet? The conversation we are having here on this page, the conversation we have been having since you opened this book, is the greatest conversation you can have. You are called to fulfill your destiny, to awaken the entrepreneur within you, to inspire the creator in you. You are called to grow beyond your comfort zone, to grow beyond your need to make a living, to grow beyond the sensations of your body, to grow beyond the small satisfactions you crave, to grow beyond anything you have ever deeply craved before.

You are here to pursue your higher aim.

You are here on this Earth to pursue this aim in your life. It is your purpose.

That is all you are here to do. It is why your soul reached out. It is your destiny.

the way to end a poem
like this
is to become suddenly quiet.

—**Charles Bukowski**
love & flame & death
Burning in Water, Drowning in Flame

Chapter 8

The Eighth Principle

A Small Business Possesses a Life of Its Own, in the Service of G-d, in Whom It Finds Reason

> *Your true place is a place of light. Even if you find yourself in the midst of darkness and sorrow, you must remember this is not your home. Your essential self lives in an inseverable bond with the Source of Light. From there it extends a glimmer of itself below to transform the darkness.*
>
> —Rabbi Menachem M. Schneerson

If, in the Seventh Principle, we are pursuing our self, in this, the Eighth Principle, we are pursuing the source of our self. We are pursuing G-d. This is the first time I have stated in any of my books that the source of our self is G-d.

To many of you, your response would be "Of course!" To many others, your response would be "Oh, no!" To still many others, your response would be "Perhaps . . . "

Whatever your response, please bear with me as we pursue the question: Why is the Most Successful Small Business in the World in the service of G-d, and why does it find reason there? And, what Michael, do you mean when you say "a life of its own"?

Let's look at these questions one at a time. First, let's address the easiest, that the Most Successful Small Business in the World lives "a life of its own."

A LIFE OF ITS OWN

There should be no doubt in your mind that the Most Successful Small Business in the World, like you, lives a life of its own. To become the Most Successful Small Business in the World, your company must possess a sense of being that expresses itself through a behavior. It must speak its own language, in a way that identifies it from all other companies—a language that identifies it as an original life form.

Every company that has achieved this measure of greatness has such a being, exhibits such behavior, and possesses such a voice.

Microsoft does. Apple does. Walmart does. McDonald's does. Yet, remarkably, each of them, as a business, sells commodities that are available in many, many forms, from many, many competitors.

How is it then, that each of the companies mentioned above has achieved the level of performance, of greatness, that it has? How is it that they have become, as each has, one of the most successful businesses in the world? What distinguishes them from all the others?

In Apple's case, it is its original voice, the look of it, the sound of it, the function of it, the feeling of it. Every customer addicted to Apple knows exactly what I mean. They could tell you, in colorful detail, why Apple stands apart from all the rest. They are in love with Apple.

In Microsoft's case, the connection is completely different. Microsoft possesses power. Microsoft possesses a power that Apple never achieved, despite how loved it is. Few people love Microsoft. Isn't that remarkable? Microsoft outpowered Apple from the very beginning. Microsoft's strategy was to achieve power, to bully the market and its competitors, to push the world around, to become the biggest guy on the block. In the process, it became the most powerful in its industry, and at the same time, the most disliked.

Apple's strategy was to be loved; to be coveted; to be charming, delightful, playful, and creative. Apple didn't stand a chance in the game Microsoft was playing. And yet, it has survived. It wasn't destroyed, as so many of its competitors were. It held its own, despite the fact that "its own" was merely a small fraction of the market that it might have possessed, had it created a different strategy. Unfortunately, Apple fell in love with itself, just as its customers had. You might say that it became a hugely narcissistic company. It became a company that looked in the pool to see its own reflection. It was a mirror of the man, Steve Jobs, who invented it. It still is, and it still does.

So, two great companies exist in the computer marketplace — Apple and Microsoft — with two completely different strategies. Each of these companies is a product of the person who created them. Each of them is a perfect mirror of the personality of its founder, Steve Jobs and Bill Gates, respectively.

Dell, of course, is a completely different story. Dell was built on the simple and straightforward strategy of going direct to its customer, providing customized solutions to each, at low cost, utilizing a standardized process to achieve that seemingly impossible result.

In Dell's case, see a door. The customer walks through the doorway, whether on the Internet, on the phone, or the door to Dell's store. This door leads them to a customer service expert. This expert is trained to quickly discover who the customer is, exactly what applications the user needs, and what features the computer must have to meet those needs, and to satisfy the user in a way that matches the user's experience, expertise, and budget. Behind the customer service expert is a vast set of shelves upon which sit the many modules, the many solutions, the many applications needed to assemble the perfect solution to the customer's needs, the customer's applications, the customer's personal pro forma, the protocol that satisfies the end result of the customer needs and wishes. See the order being placed for the specialized-albeit-standardized product that Dell will assemble after the order is paid for and placed. See the customized Dell solution going through the assembly plant, where it is made ready to go out the door. See the FedEx trucks awaiting the shipment to the customer, who will receive it in short order, exactly as promised, exactly as anticipated.

Dell is a system. A system designed to satisfy its customers, each and every one of them, no matter how inexperienced or experienced they are. You can find a Dell computer in the hands of a specialist or a novice. The computer doesn't care. The computer was built for the individual user; one computer does not fit all.

In that way, Dell differentiated itself from all of its competitors by understanding the customer's frustrations and desires and then satisfying them in a way, and at a price, that no other computer company had ever done.

In a way, that's exactly what Burger King did to differentiate itself from McDonald's. "Have it your way!" Burger King said. Again, see the customer walk through the door, walk up to the counter, and place a special order for a standardized, customized product—their hamburger, exactly the way they want it, but at a price far lower than that which they would have to pay in a normal restaurant, where you would expect exactly the same thing. Of course, at McDonald's, you wouldn't expect to have it "your way"—you would expect to have it McDonald's way. And given that McDonald's way created a revolution in the restaurant industry, everyone who went there did so because they had grown to love the McDonald's way. They had grown to expect it.

And of course we have Walmart. Walmart is the most maligned *and* the most successful business of its kind in the world.

Obviously, despite the negative press, there is a following of consumers who are crazy about Walmart. Walmart hires tens of thousands of employees; they serve tens of millions of customers. Walmart grows exponentially each year, beyond where they were the year before.

How does Walmart manage to do what they do? How do they manage to select the multi-millions of products they choose for their stores? How do they manage to provide those products in their multi-thousands of stores, with such predictability, and with such unbelievable control? How do they manage to create the

Walmart story every day in every way so consistently, so impeccably, that their millions of customers continue to select Walmart as the one place they shop, continuously, to make their ordinary purchases in their extraordinary way?

Each of these companies—Apple, Microsoft, Walmart, Dell, McDonald's, and many more—became, each in its own way, the most successful small business in the world. They discovered—*created*—their own way of becoming the singular story, in their own very singular world, in their very own singular way, and they possess a life of their own.

If you were to be invited to live inside of those companies, to be a part of those companies, to discover the soul of those companies, you would know the truth of their singularity. You would know the truth of their very personal, very creative, very individual form.

IN THE SERVICE OF G-D

This speaks to a conversation that may not be so obvious but that is critical to the subject at hand.

In each of the cases above, the founders—the entrepreneurs—were called to create an enterprise so far beyond the ordinary that to even contemplate it called for energy that few of us have ever experienced.

The scale of these companies is beyond our imagination. And, just so, the energy required to even imagine creating such a thing, is beyond our imagination.

We, all of us, are completely consumed, trying to live our lives, our ordinary lives, our trying to "make a living" lives, our trying to pay our mortgage lives, our trying to raise our kids lives, our trying to be a good husband or wife lives, our trying to get on and get by lives. How in the world, with all we do, each and every hour of each and every day, could we even imagine the possibility of creating a worldwide phenomenon, as each of those companies have done?

And, if we cannot conceive of such a phenomenon, how can we conceive of G-d?

I woke up several mornings ago, with this question in my mind, in a way that it has rarely come to me. This question relates to the inability to feel G-d. In my dream, I had a conversation with a friend about loving G-d, my inability to do that, my inability to even imagine how to do that. I imagine that must have been the fuel to feed that thought, as I woke up with the question: If G-d exists, *and I am absolutely certain that G-d does exist*, how could I possibly relate to that reality? How could I possibly understand what G-d is?

I had decided many months ago that this chapter had to appear in this book, that the Eighth Principle was a challenge that we all had to address. I knew that I couldn't write a book about entrepreneurship, about the Most Successful Small Business in the World, if I didn't address this subject—the subject of G-d in the creation of the very best business in the world.

But, what do I say, and how should I say it?

When I woke up on that particular morning, I came to the realization that the subject of G-d, let alone the reality of G-d, is beyond my ability to express. It is beyond our ability to understand. My mind couldn't deal with it. It couldn't deal with what it means to see the creation of everything that is, to understand the creation of all that is, to understand what must possibly be true about G-d, Who was and is before everything that exists—the planets, the universe, the stars, the black holes, the galaxies, and the endless array of everything that one could see in a telescope or a microscope. You and I cannot truly understand the sheer overwhelming extraordinariness of it all. How in the world, and without the world, can we, could we, possibly understand what, who, G-d is?

It was not that my mind cannot encompass it; it's that the totality of me cannot even begin to *relate* to it. The only thing left, the only thing I felt, was this incredible sense of awe.

And even as I say this to you, I feel like a child . . . A child, in childhood, at that time in my life when I first contemplated the subject of G-d.

When I was a child, in my synagogue as a young Jewish boy, I could not relate my rabbi, or the congregation, or my mother and my father and my brother and my sisters to the subject of G-d. How could I make that connection? The rabbi and the congregation were so ordinary. My mother and my father and my brother and my sisters were all so ordinary, so uninspiring, so trivial. And so was I. I felt what it means to be a human being. I felt what it means to get up in the morning, the feelings I had that something was missing, and I didn't know what it was.

But, it was G-d.

I know that now.

It was G-d.

We talked about G-d, we pretended we prayed to G-d, we pretended we believed in G-d, but we didn't live our lives with the awe of G-d. We didn't experience the immensity—*beyond immensity*—of G-d, the incomprehensible question of G-d. How could G-d be, we never asked. We simply accepted, because our religion told us to, that G-d exists, that G-d created the world, that G-d is.

But, what does that mean?

What does it mean that G-d "is?"

How can you and I come anywhere close to the idea that G-d "is?"

And why is that important to the question we are asking about the Most Successful Small Business in the World?

We must ask this question. I realize this. To create the Most Successful Small Business in the World, we must ask the most important question in the world, which is the question of G-d.

We must ask that question because the Ten Principles demand it of us. The Ten Principles demand that we think bigger, act bigger, and persist longer, than any ordinary business would ask us to do.

We must ask these questions of ourselves, of the people we hire, of the investors we inspire, in order to create the most extraordinary result any human being has ever created in the history of the world.

We must rise above ourselves. We must rise above what it means to be human. We must rise above what our ordinary consciousness inspires us to do. We must rise above our needs, our self-interest, our greed, our hunger. We must pursue the impossible in everything we do. We must ask ourselves the question, What would G-d have us do?

Imagine if we took that question seriously. Imagine if we took that question to heart.

What would G-d have us do?

I was bar mitzvahed 60 years ago.

The picture of my bar mitzvah with my mother, Helen, and my father, Harry, hangs now above my computer as I write this to you. I see their smiling faces. I see my smiling face. I remember the navy blue sports jacket I wore on that day. I can see it in the picture. I remember how proud my father was that day. I can see it in the picture. I remember how thrilled I was that day, at 13 years old, that I had completed my study, I had performed my service, I had made my parents happy, and yet, in that picture, where was G-d?

I know as I speak to you now, that G-d was there. But, I also know that none of us in that picture *knew* that G-d was there. And perhaps some of the people, our family, our friends, our members of the community, knew that G-d was there, but I couldn't see them. I couldn't. Not then. Not during the entire preparation. Not after that picture was taken. Was G-d in the picture? And I ask you today, why couldn't I see Him? What needed to occur for me to see G-d then? To see G-d when I woke up that very morning? To see G-d every day during the 60 years that followed that singular event?

And what would have happened if we *had* seen G-d in that picture, with that young, smiling boy, that mother, that father, those members of that Jewish community?

I say to you, everything would have happened.

I say to you, everything *could* have happened.

I say to you, we must ask this question.

AND THIS IS MY BELIEF

To conceive of a company of 10,000 stores, or of a company like Apple, Microsoft, Dell, McDonald's, or Walmart, being excited about business is insufficient. It is insufficient for you to believe in a secular reality. It is insufficient for you to want to make a lot of money, to become financially independent, to be excited at all. To conceive of a company of 10,000 stores, what I am calling the Most Successful Small Business in the World, you must be moved by a higher cause than is grounded in you. You are not enough. You are never enough. You are not simply the product of personal growth. To even contemplate this great thing we are conceiving of here, you must be touched by the original maker, the source of all sources, which we are calling G-d, defined as the infinite source of all. I am not talking about religion, of course; I am talking about the source of all religion. I am talking about what was missing in my bar mitzvah, and what was missing in the picture. I am talking about what was missing in my life, despite the unchallengeable fact that of course G-d was always there. If He had not been there, we would not be here. If He had not been present in that picture, there would be no picture for G-d to be present in. If G-d were not present in the founders of the great companies I listed above, there would not be the possibility of the great companies I listed above. If G-d is not present in your heart, in your imagination, in your desire to create the Most Successful Small Business in the World, the *possibility* of creating the Most Successful Small Business in the World would not exist.

See it.

Go back to before the beginning.

Go back to where there was just G-d.

Go back to just before the immensity beyond immensity beyond any word that you can use to describe that immensity, of the creation of the universe, our world, all things we see and those things we don't see. Go back and attempt to understand what G-d is, was, will always be. There is no way you can imagine such a reality. There is only the sense of extreme awe, amazement, astonishment, and bewilderment that arises in you, at the center of you, when you even contemplate such a thing.

There is only the question: How can that be?

Imagine how deathly the soul of a human being would be if that question had been answered with, "There is no G-d. There is only man, and evolution, and the science of life, not the miracle of life." Imagine how that would affect your dream, your vision, your purpose, your mission.

Experience the question: How can that be?

Experience the experience of asking that question.

Experience the soul of your self as you ask that question earnestly, as a little child might, and did.

Ask yourself what that little child in you experienced as he, as she, came to the question about G-d, about the amazement, the mystery, the astonishment, the joy, the wonder of G-d in your child mind, in your child heart, in your child imagination.

That is what is called for in the creation of the Most Successful Small Business in the World. That is what gives birth to every unique human being. That is what gives birth to the most successful small business in the world. What would G-d have you do?

a life can change in a tenth of
a second
or sometimes it can take
70
years.

> —Charles Bukowski
> *you tell me what it means*
> *The Flash of Lightning Behind the Mountain*

Chapter 9

The Ninth Principle

A Small Business Is an Economic Entity, Driving an Economic Reality, Creating an Economic Certainty for the Communities in Which It Thrives

If money is your hope for independence you will never have it. The only real security that a man will have in this world is a reserve of knowledge, experience, and ability.

—Henry Ford

And then there's money. Money has become the economic reality of the world. It is *the* economic necessity that all people in the world must deal with, define for themselves, and come to terms with, whether they wish to or not. The Most Successful Small Business in the World must also deal with this question, if it is to become what it presumes to become. If it fails to deal with this question, or if it does so in a self-centered manner, it will fail. It will fail, just as all businesses that unsuccessfully deal with money ultimately fail. But when we come to understand the Ninth Principle, we see that money is not the issue at all. Money is the economic reality that we in business choose to address, or fail to address. The consequence of this action, or inaction, will help us succeed or make us fail. The Ninth Principle says that money is simply a company's fuel. Money is the fuel that generates the energy of imagination, the energy of growth, the energy of development, the energy of life. Your company creates your economy, the Ninth Principle says; your economy does not create your company. Money does not create money, despite what all the "money people" say. Money is fuel and only fuel. Money is simply the fuel that feeds energy. That energy, in turn, feeds the outcome which is born of your imagination, which is what fuels the development of the product of your imagination.

Think about it this way. Seventy percent of all companies in the United States are sole proprietorships. That means one person—the owner, the sole supplier, the sole operator.

Imagine for the moment that each of those sole proprietors were to hire five people. Only five. What would that mean to the economy of the community in which that company had decided to grow beyond the purview of only one person? The economy would have grown five times! Think about that for the moment. What would it mean if a community in which 10,000 sole proprietorships had grown five times? What would the financial impact of that be? What would it mean if you decided to create the Most Successful Small Business in the World, the intent of which would be to invent a way to grow every sole proprietorship five times its original size? And to do so successfully! What would the impact of your company be on the world? What would occur if, in fact, you realized your dream, the dream of five times? What would happen if you spread your dream worldwide, so that in every country in the world, every sole proprietorship, every self employed individual, was inspired to grow five times his or her current size? Only five times. Not 50 times. Not 150 times. Not 10,000 times! But only five times. What would be the significance of that decision you had made? What would you need to do to manifest that decision into reality? Well, of course, you would have to figure out how to attract every sole proprietor in the world to talk to you. To have them listen to what you had to say. To be interested in the possibility of growing five times his or her company's size. You would have to create a story that demonstrates the five times phenomenon, which is transforming the world. You would have to design a system that would make it relatively easy for your sole proprietor clients to achieve that objective, the objective of five times. You would then be able to demonstrate to your five times clients that once they learned the secret of five times, they could then replicate their five times company another 25 times, by teaching it to five new five times sole proprietors, who in turn would grow their company five times. They would then be able to replicate their five times phenomenon 25 times by licensing other sole proprietors to do the very same thing. They in turn could grow their company 25 times, and on and on and on.

See the five times phenomenon growing from community to community throughout the world.

See the simple start of it; the simple realization of it. Ask yourself what the five times system would need to possess, in order for it to work, just like McDonald's did and does. See the economic combustion of it, the economic miracle of it. See the profound impact that it would have on the world.

IT'S NOT THE MONEY, STUPID

The money is the easy part. Do not believe the current administration in Washington, DC, which seeks to convince the American people that the money is the hardest part and that's why we need our government to fund our lives. They would have us believe that we *need* them to fund our insurance, to fund our mortgages, to fund our energy, to fund our retirement. They seek to convince us that our financial problems are so *huge*, that *only* the government is big enough to deal with it. The vast majority, who have never understood money, never understood self-sufficiency, never understood what it means to awaken the entrepreneur within, have bought into our government's story, the story that put us—in fewer than 200 days—into $10 trillion of debt. Because we don't understand money or where it actually comes from and because we don't feel competent to invent our own personal transformational economy, we have bought into the belief that the financial problem is actually bigger than all of us, and therefore can be addressed only by those who govern us. And in the process, we have given up control of our financial future to those who will design it for us, divine it for us, as though we are all too poor—too intellectually poor, too creatively poor, too energetically poor, too financially poor—to do it for ourselves.

What a crime our government has committed. What a crime we, the "too poor," have committed by allowing them to do this to us, to our country. What a crime we have committed by our lack of interest in pursuing our own story, the creation of America. Our founders left us the keys to a solid financial future, by designing a republic in which all the rules were created on the basis of freedom. That freedom was bequeathed to each and every one of us. We were given the freedom to choose our own life's path. We were given the freedom to create, and the freedom to imagine, beyond anything we have ever created or imagined before.

That's why I say to you that this is the age of the new entrepreneur. Imagine, just imagine, the five times phenomenon I just shared with you was a venture for real. Just imagine that you decided that you could figure out how to attract sole proprietors, inspire sole proprietors, teach sole proprietors, train sole proprietors, coach sole proprietors, transform sole proprietors, to become entrepreneurial leaders in their community. Just imagine that the five times phenomenon was something you could actually create! Then what? What would you be able to do with it? What would the economic impact of it be on our struggling, yes, disastrous economy? What would the government be able to do then? What could they do, would they do if all sole proprietors became converts to the five times system, living a five times life? Do you understand that's all Ray Kroc did at McDonald's? That's all Sam Walton did at Walmart? That's all Michael Dell did at Dell? That's all Steve Jobs did at Apple? That's all Bill Gates did at Microsoft? And because it's so simple, you can do it too. What's your five times solution to the problems that beset the more than 6 billion suffering people in the world? What is your 10,000 stores solution? What is your simple, predictable method for transforming the economic reality in every human being's life? Do you see how simple it really is? Do you see, for example, that you could do the same thing with the insurance business, where every insurance agent who is operating as a sole proprietor could suddenly see the future, his future, her future, in a five times way? Do you see that this simple idea, expressed correctly, imaginatively, productively, authentically—just this silly little idea—could transform the economic reality of your world, the world of people around you, the world of people around them? Just five times!

No, it's not "the money, stupid." It's the idea.

I watch the best Broadway musical
from the best seat in the house
and I am the author and the critic and the
audience and sometimes I'm on stage
too.

—Charles Bukowski
the wavering line
The Flash of Lightning Behind the Mountain

Chapter 10

The Tenth Principle

A Small Business Creates a Standard Against Which All Small Businesses Are Measured as Either Successful, or Not, to Upgrade the Possibility for All Small Businesses to Thrive Beyond the Standards That Formerly Existed, Whether Stated or Not

It's tough. We're probably holding ourselves to a higher standard than we may be ready for but at this institution you have to do that.

—Billy Lange

Well, yes, that is a mouthful. But, let's look at it more closely so that you can interpret what is meant by "standards."

According to the *New Oxford American Dictionary*, a standard is an agreed upon "level of quality or attainment."

Simple, yes? But, it is not so simple when you study the subject of small business (or *all* business for that matter). You will discover that there are few, if any, agreed-upon standards that define the operating effectiveness and/or efficiency, let alone morality and quality to be expected of any and all businesses.

While establishing the Ten Principles for inventing the Most Successful Small Business in the World, the outcome of our work together must be, as said here in the Tenth Principle, to establish the standards by which your company will be evaluated objectively, in order to attain the status of above-world-class performance.

These standards will be, as already stated: visual, emotional, functional, and financial. They will include a company's verifiable ability to transform its customer's life, by delivering a quantifiably determinable result, beyond that of any other company in its market. They will also include a company's verifiable ability to scale, such as to grow, in a determinedly replicable manner. These standards will raise the bar of expectations for any and every small company, should that company profess to be a growth company, determined to become the Most Successful Small Business in the World. In short, any company that is uninterested in becoming the Most Successful Small Business in the World would be measured by these standards. But, all companies, no matter where they find themselves on the growth curve, would be affected by this measure.

Let's take these standards apart and revisit them.

THE STANDARDS DETERMINED TO BE ABOVE WORLD CLASS

World-class standards are easily identified.

- The *visual standards* of cleanliness, of order, of color, of harmony, of balance, of serendipity. All of these things are so clearly and effortlessly imaginable and demonstrably important to the effect one wishes to create. All are, of course, components of a world-class company.

- The *emotional standards* of happiness, excitement, joy, camaraderie, caring, empathy, courage, and consistency are obviously essential for a world-class company.

- The *functional standards* of a world-class company are also quite obvious. They are simply the means through which your company makes a promise and keeps it, a promise that is beyond that of a normal business, struggling to get by day to day.

- The *financial standards* are equally self-evident in a world-class company. Pricing is lower, profits are higher, return on investment is greater, and cash flow is consistent.

Above-world-class standards are less obvious, and therefore most essential for the Most Successful Small Business in the World.

Above-world-class standards include all of the above but take them to a degree rarely experienced in a business of any kind. These above-world-class standards include spiritual standards, psychological standards, ethical standards, and philosophical standards.

BORDERS
BOOKS MUSIC AND CAFE
1750 29th STREET, #1052
BOULDER, CO 80301
720-565-8266

STORE: 0407   REG: 03/58   TRAN#: 0950
SALE   01/17/2010   EMP: 00304

MOST SUCCESSFUL SMALL BUSINESS
        9961344   CL T   16.72
  24.95 33% BR PROMO
COUPON 159045010000000000

                Subtotal   16.72
BR: 8301791672

                Subtotal   16.72
                COLORADO 8.16%   1.36
 1 Item   Total   18.08
                VISA   18.08
ACCT # /S XXXXXXXXXXXXX9056
                 AUTH: 01112B
NAME: KELLY/GIL

You Saved $8.23

        01/17/2010 05:40PM

Shop online
24 hours a day
at Borders.com

purchase price will be refunded in the form of a return gift card.

Exchanges of opened audio books, music, videos, video games, software and electronics will be permitted subject to the same time periods and receipt requirements as above and can be made for the same item only.

Periodicals, newspapers, comic books, food and drink, digital downloads, gift cards, return gift cards, items marked "non-returnable," "final sale" or the like and out-of-print, collectible or pre-owned items cannot be returned or exchanged.

Returns and exchanges to a Borders, Borders Express or Waldenbooks retail store of merchandise purchased from Borders.com may be permitted in certain circumstances. See Borders.com for details.

BORDERS.

Returns

Returns of merchandise purchased from a borders, Borders Express or Waldenbooks retail store will be permitted only if presented in saleable condition accompanied by the original sales receipt or Borders gift receipt within the time periods specified below. Returns accompanied by the original sales receipt must be made within 30 days of purchase and the purchase price will be refunded in the same form as the original purchase. Returns accompanied by the original Borders gift receipt must be made within 60 days of purchase and the purchase price will be refunded in the form of a return gift card.

Exchanges of opened audio books, music, videos, video games, software and electronics will be permitted subject to the same time periods and receipt requirements as above and can be made for the same item only.

Periodicals, newspapers, comic books, food and drink

STORE: 0407   REG: 03/58   TRAN#: 0950
SALE   01/17/2010   EMP: 00304

digital downloads, gift cards, return gift cards, items marked "non-returnable," "final sale" or the like and out-of-print, collectible or pre-owned items cannot be returned or exchanged.

Returns and exchanges to a Borders, Borders Express or Waldenbooks retail store of merchandise purchased from Borders.com may be permitted in certain circumstances. See Borders.com for details.

BORDERS.

Returns

Returns of merchandise purchased from a Borders, Borders Express or Waldenbooks retail store will be permitted only if presented in saleable condition accompanied by the original sales receipt or Borders gift receipt within the time periods specified below. Returns accompanied by the original sales receipt must be made within 30 days of purchase and the purchase price will be refunded in the same form as the original purchase. Returns accompanied by the original Borders gift receipt must be made within 60 days of purchase and the purchase price will be refunded in the form of a return gift card.

Exchanges of opened audio books, music, videos, video games, software and electronics will be permitted subject to the same time periods and receipt requirements as above and can be made for the same item only.

Periodicals, newspapers, comic books, food and drink, digital downloads, gift cards, return gift cards, items marked "non-returnable," "final sale" or the like and out-of-print, collectible or pre-owned items cannot be returned or exchanged.

Returns and exchanges to a Borders, Borders Express or Waldenbooks retail store of merchandise purchased from Borders.com may be permitted in certain circumstances. See Borders.com for details.

Spiritual standards are related to the human spirit or soul.

Psychological standards are related to the state of mind of your people, the inferences through which they come to their decisions, and the spin they put on their motives the motives of others.

Ethical standards are related to the choices that your company and your people make, the justification for those choices, the morality underlying them, and the effect those choices have on others, both within your company and outside of it.

Philosophical standards relate to the belief system or worldview held by your company. This determines the decisions, attitudes, and mind-set upon which your company's decisions are made.

Let's take a closer look at each.

SPIRITUAL STANDARDS

What is the soul? What does the soul of your company know and do? Can it be said that there is a soul of your company? Do companies possess a life of their own?

The soul is the spirit or immaterial part of us, the essence that makes us who we are. It is the energy that moves us to make the choices we make, through our psychological framework, and through the social system we participate in as individuals. In short, we are born with a soul already within us, and that soul shapes and is shaped by the circumstances and conditions that surround us throughout our lives. Our soul expresses itself through our communication or lack of it, through our decision or indecision, through our relationships or detachments. Our soul can be damaged, debilitated, enhanced, aroused, and inspired by thought. Our soul is affected by thoughts of our own, thoughts of others. Our soul is affected by our own actions and those of others.

Just so, your company has a soul. Your company is born with a soul. At the center of it, is the founder's soul or the founders' souls. The providers of capital to your company impact either positively or negatively upon the soul of your company. They shrink the potential of your company's spirit or its soul, or inspire it to go beyond itself. They enhance your company's soul or diminish your company's soul.

The leaders and managers of your company also impact either positively or negatively upon the soul of your company. If the leaders or managers in your company are disinterested in the subject of "soul," they will kill the idea of "soul" in your company. Killing the idea of "soul" in your company thus *deadens* the soul of your company! A CEO I knew not that long ago referred to such a conversation as "touchy feely" with such distaste that I wondered where he had been living for the past 54 years of his life. The answer of course was obvious: He had been living in a soul-less family, going to a soul-less school, working in soul-less companies, furthering his soul-less mind-set, which ordained all things of soul to a world he didn't, nor cared to, live in.

Spiritual standards regard the use of language and behavior as a soulful context from which all decisions are made. The question, "What is the soul of our company?" is an essential question for soulful entrepreneurs, but most importantly for the founder of the Most Successful Small Business in the World. The soul of success is a vibrant soul, a sensitive soul, a brilliant soul, an adventurous soul, a playful soul, an inquisitive (rather than acquisitive) soul, a soul that asks the meaningful questions even when faced with a seemingly meaningless world.

This then defines the spiritual standard of your company. A company that believes in G-d, in a higher cause, in a cause beyond the human, that puts the human context within a context of awe, of love, of the search for your company's holy grail. "Beyond human" does not mean that the human component of your company is lessened by the context of G-d. Rather, it creates greater meaning to what it means to human, greater responsibility for the human effect of your company. It increases your company's humanness, its life force, and its drive to rise above the merely human, to become the highest a human can accede to, the essence of an ascending soul.

PSYCHOLOGICAL STANDARDS

The *psychology* of humankind, or of your company, is not the *spirituality* of humanity or of your company. The psychology of humankind is highly impacted by spirituality, but the two are quite different. The psychology of humans and of your company is the product of your soul meeting and relating to the world. The impact of the world on your soul, and the transformation of your soul into a living human being, comprises a marriage of the Divine with the animal. It is the marriage of the divine soul and the animal soul. This, of course, is only my interpretation of this thought, not my creation of this thought. But, in my mind, the divine soul is that part of us which aspires to G-d, while the animal soul is that part of us which is brought to life by our body, and the senses that move it. The divine soul is that part of us which would bring heaven to Earth. The animal soul is that part of us which regards Earth—all of our senses that drive and please us—as "heaven." Or, as the case might be, "hell."

The psychology of humankind that comprises the psychology of your company is the synthesis of the two. The question is then which drives your company more, your earthly passions or your divine passions? Or both? Well, of course it is both, because we *are* both. The larger question then is what is the balance between the two? How is that balance reflected in your company, or more accurately, the psychological health of your company? If the psychology of your company is driven by greed, the psychology of your company will be apparent on its face. The greed will reveal itself in every action of your company, as we've just experienced on Wall Street. The greed I'm speaking of is not simply the greed for money, but the greed for power. The greed of our current administration in Washington, DC, is just as apparent as the greed on Wall Street that created the financial devastation we've all suffered. The greed in Washington, DC, of course, is the greed for power. The financial implications of that greed will have an even more profoundly negative impact on us than the greed of its predecessors. Our willingness to give our lives over to Washington, DC's greed for power is another sort of psychological imbalance. This imbalance will be reflected in your company, should it give itself up to benefits perceived to be derived from an increasingly beneficent government, no matter what the cost to others. I had a partner who came to me incredibly excited by the "free money" that the government willed into being for anyone smart enough to take advantage of it. "Why would we do that?" I asked him. "Because we can!" he answered. "It's the biggest single opportunity for small business in three decades!" he continued. "But who's paying for it?" I asked him. "Who cares?" he remarked. "Goodbye," I said to my partner. Think about it. Is that the psychology of the company you want to create? Is that likely that a company founded upon the principle of "free money" will become the Most Successful Small Business in the World? Is that how a truly entrepreneurial individual would care to be remembered? Does he want to be remembered because he was clever? Does he want to be known for someone who used what was available, despite the fact that someone else was going to have to pay for it? That *you* would end up paying for it?

What are the psychological standards to which your company would adhere?

One would be equity—that whatever decisions you make would be fair. Another would be empathy—that the lives of the people you do business with would be understood and highly regarded.

Another would be tolerance—that the mistakes of others would be seen for what they are. Mistakes in judgment. Mistakes in understanding. Mistakes in skill. Mistakes in belief.

Another would be aspiration—that your decisions would always conform to the highest objectives, as opposed to the meanest objectives.

Think of your company as you would a mature and balanced human being. What would such a person aspire to, practice, become, in his relationship with himself and the world?

ETHICAL STANDARDS

The difficulty that we have when we speak of soul, psychology, ethics, and philosophy is that when taken apart they sound very similar to each other. However similar they may sound, they are derived in a completely different way. You are born with a soul, which is then either enhanced or debilitated. You develop a psychology, either intentionally or through the influences that surround you, both within you and within your world. When it comes to ethics, however, they are both absolute and relative. They existed before all time and they exist within time. Ethics, yours and those of your company—your community, your government, your world—are derived from tradition, religion, law, and community, and, as I've implied earlier, from G-d. The aggregation of these absolute and relative ethics, and the assimilation of them within your company, must be formulated within your company intentionally. They must be stated unequivocally in a document called, as they are called in the United States of America, our company's bill of rights, our company's constitution.

What is in the bill of rights of the Most Successful Small Business in the World? What does the constitution of the Most Successful Small Business in the World say? What tenets do we hold to, fast and firmly? What position does our company take in the world? What do our founders say? What do they commit this company to? What position do they take in the world, in this age of the new entrepreneur?

If you have not read the United States of America Constitution or its Bill of Rights lately, please do so. Read them and ask these questions of yourself: How would I behave if I were a founder of this country, with this company I am about to create? What expectations would I have? What moral codes would I adopt to represent its interactions with my customers, my suppliers, my investors, my employees? What expectations would I have if I knew that in the establishment of the Most Successful Small Business in the World—with the actual creation of it— that I am establishing an ethical template for all businesses in the world? For every business in the world? In every country in the world? What if I could believe that, deeply in my heart, I am a soul created by G-d to bring heaven to Earth? It is my accountability—my destiny—to think this through as though the world depended upon me, upon my company, upon the thoughtfulness I will expend in the creation of it? The ethical standards of your company will determine whether it will become the great company we're speaking about here. It is the foundation upon which your company will be built.

PHILOSOPHICAL STANDARDS

Philosophy asks the question, Where does knowledge exist? That is, how do we know what we know? To be complete, your company, the Most Successful Small Business in the World, must ask that question, and then formulate an answer to it. In one sense, your constitution and bill of rights are an answer to the philosophical question. In another way, they aren't. They are the answer to that question because through your constitution and bill of rights you are saying: This is what we believe. But, in another way, they are not the answer to the philosophical question because your constitution and bill of rights do not tell us the foundation of those beliefs. In my book, *Awakening the Entrepreneur Within,* I define the process through which one awakens the spirit of entrepreneurship through the creation of a dream, a vision, a purpose, and a mission. I go on to say that the dream is the product of the dreamer. The vision is the product of the thinker. The purpose is the product of the storyteller. And the mission is the product of the leader. Each of those four entrepreneurial personalities—dreamer, thinker, storyteller, and leader—plays a role in the creation and growth of an entrepreneurially driven company.

The dreamer creates the dream, the thinker the vision, the storyteller the purpose, and the leader the mission. Although they seem to be four different people, they are instead four essential components of the entrepreneur. The creations—dream, vision, purpose, and mission—work together toward the manifestation of the dream, a company whose purpose it is to transform one aspect of the world, which becomes the product of the entrepreneur's passion. The four dimensions of the entrepreneur then become a process through which the end game is realized. Without the vision, the dream would become a fantasy. Without the purpose, the vision would have no meaning. Without the mission, there would be no pragmatic value to the process. In other words, the dream drives the passion forward; the vision creates a picture of what form it will take; the purpose tells us for whom and why it is all being done; the mission provides us with the details essential to "putting the pieces together" in such a way that each of the four components preceding it are realized.

By describing that model to you, I am essentially describing my philosophy to you—that all things play a part in the creation of all things. That the universe is one thing, and that nothing can be done without affecting everything else. And, by another course of thinking, if you leave something out, the same result is true— nothing affects everything. Whether by commission or omission, you cannot invent a company that is anything other than a sum of its parts or, equally, its nonparts. What is left out is left in because of its absence. This leads to my conclusion that the company you are inventing, the Most Successful Small Business in the World, is a system of interlocking and interrelated parts. Each of these parts spells out the personality of your company, each of which is a voice within the voice of your company, and, if any of the parts were gone from the picture, would create a completely different company.

I think that way because it *is* that way. It is that way because I *think* that way. And I think that way so that my company must *behave* that way; if it failed to *behave* that way, then my thoughts would be meaningless. If my thoughts are meaningless, then I am meaningless, because my thoughts are me and I am my thoughts. Just as your thoughts are you and you are your thoughts. Not solely our thoughts, of course, but meaningfully we are our thoughts. Our thoughts create our feelings and our feelings create our thoughts, and our senses create both. Our thoughts and our feelings create our senses, or shape them in a way that they would not be shaped had we been created differently.

Seeing the sun, one might say, would be a different experience by each and every person who would see it. Expressing that vision would be different for each and every. A picture of the sun would be painted differently by each and every one of us. In the painting of the sun, we, the painters, are communicating to everyone else how the sun appears to us, feels to us . . . and only to us. Van Gogh's sun is different from Rembrandt's sun. Michelangelo's David is different from Picasso's David. And yet, the sun, the one sun that we are all describing in our way, your way, my way, is, and will always be, the one sun we are all speaking about; the absolute sun, as opposed to the relative sun. So, your company is your sun and my company is my sun, and the Most Successful Small Business in the World is the sun of who creates it. That is a philosophical conversation. Your company will be enriched or bedeviled by the philosophical standards you establish for it. This will happen, whether by choice or by accident.

Some people never go crazy.
What truly horrible lives
They must lead.

—Charles Bukowski
some people
Burning in Water, Drowning in Flame

Concerning Success

So now we've arrived at the beginning, at the end, that is, at the end of this book and at the beginning of your work. You're looking into the mirror of our present, past, and future relationship.

What have we learned together?

How do you apply the Ten Principles?

How do you go to work *on* your new enterprise or the company you created many months ago, rather than so dutifully, earnestly—as everybody so wrongfully does—going to work *in* it?

Are you truly about to invent the Most Successful Small Business in the World? Are you as serious about this as I am? Or do you believe that my conversation with you has been a metaphorical one?

Here's the thing: There is no other option available for you to pursue!

Not unless you are determined to disappoint yourself. There is no other option for you to pursue other than to pursue the great one, the imaginative one, the declaration of your own independence.

Your life is now on the line. Because you've come this far. Because you've read through what I wrote, just for you. Because you've taken me seriously, and now you must take yourself seriously too. Otherwise, you wouldn't be here. You would have quit long ago, at Chapter 1 or Chapter 2.

There is no other way we could be having this conversation. Do you realize that yet? That you are now obligated to awaken the entrepreneur within you in the most serious way, in this age of the new entrepreneur? That it is you, the new entrepreneur—the dreamer, the thinker, the storyteller, the leader. The new entrepreneur. Just like Muhammad Yunus is.

You are an amazing individual. Fearful just like the rest of us. Confused, of course. And excited beyond belief.

You have no way of knowing how to start, no matter what you have done before. You have no way of knowing what you're getting yourself involved in, of course. Because creating the Most Successful Small Business in the World has never been discussed with you before this. You have never even thought it to be possible. Because, in many ways, it is not possible. It's a stretch for even the most imaginative of us to believe it to be possible.

But, here we are. Here we are. And it is indeed possible.

Stop for a moment. Stop thinking for a moment. Come to grips with this possibility. The Ten Principles will guide you. They will always serve as the cornerstone, the foundation for the work you are about to do. They were written for that purpose. When you are in doubt, the Ten Principles will remind you that there is no need to doubt, only the need to create.

Put your mind and heart to the wheel of your imagination. Roll forward. There is no other place to go, but forward. And as you do, your imagination will conceive of, deliberate on, conceptualize, and formulate something beyond you.

The Most Successful Small Business in the World is simply waiting there in its unimaginable perfection in your heart and in your mind and in the world.

The people you are here to serve have been waiting, without realizing it, for what you are going to give them, provide them, and create for them. They are unconsciously willing you to move forward. Their desire can be felt if you allow yourself to feel it.

Just imagine, just imagine . . .

Just allow yourself to imagine, to engage yourself, to inspire yourself, to create yourself.

This is the beginning, not the end. This is the beginning of the great result you are about to pursue.

This is not a theoretical conversation. We are not in school. This is the product of an intense, purposeful life, which has been engaged in the reality of small business, participating in the lives of tens of thousands of small business owners. Engaged with those who would be entrepreneurs, but had no way of knowing the right way until we engaged, seriously engaged, in this meaningful conversation.

I have had hundreds of thousands of these serious conversations. I have had these conversations with people who had launched their business in exactly the wrong way. With people who told me that if they had known what I had shared with them at the very beginning of their business, they would have not wasted so much of their life. They would not have worked so impossibly hard, would not have had so many painful mind-bruising experiences.

Now you and I have created a platform for all the work you are about to do, the platform I call the Ten Principles. The Ten Principles will save your life, on the way to saving so many others' lives.

And that's why you and I are here. To save other people's lives. While saving our own.

This is not a theoretical conversation. No, it's not theoretical at all. This is not a classroom. This is not a school. This is not for your entertainment. This is for you and your world. Our world.

WHEN WE BEGIN SOMETHING, WE BEGIN IT

Or we're not truly in it. This is the start of your great idea. This is the romance, the sweet song, the passionate connection with your heart, with the soul that breathes fire in you, to rise higher within you, to inspire within you, to touch the lover within you, to feel the kiss of your imagination within you, to breathe so deeply within you that you can hardly breathe at all within you.

How else to describe it? When the idea comes to you, without announcing itself to you—just arrives within you, with such an amazing light within you—how would you describe it?

Yes, I am talking about you, even if you might think at this moment that I'm talking about someone else, about something else, other than business. Can this actually be a conversation about business? Can this actually be a business thought, a business relationship, a business worth pursuing?

Have we gone off the deep edge? Oh, yes. Oh, without a doubt. Without a doubt, we have taken a leap into a world in which business doesn't speak. In which business doesn't have a voice. A leap into a world where the pragmatic is so emphatic as to be emblematic of old thoughts. Old Joseph. You remember him. Old company. You remember it. Old ideas. You remember how they came about. Old wisdom. Not the kind to truck about.

But now we're here, you and I, dear friend. We are stretching our spiritual wings. We are daring to go beyond the obvious. We are daring to challenge the academic. We are daring to chase away the stereotypes, of beliefs, of prejudices, of form, of circumstances, of male, of female, of parenting, of the conditions which ensnare us.

When we begin something, we truly begin it, or we're not earnestly in it. Which means, as I've said, a blank piece of paper and beginner's mind . . . or nothing.

We cannot truly begin this thing if we have done it before. We cannot truly begin this thing if it's only a reflection of an old idea. We cannot truly begin this thing if we have done it all before. Or if it's simply a reflection of someone else's idea. Or if it's simply a device to generate wealth. What in the world would you do with wealth if you earned it? What purpose would it truly serve? Your own? Is that enough? Does that fulfill your purpose on Earth? Does that fill your soul?

Which is what I say to you, dear reader. As we come to the end, and begin the beginning.

With love.

An Invitation From The Author

As I said in the introduction of this book, I want to speak to you, and to hear you speak.

I want to know you, and to know what is important to you.

I want to engage with you, and to have you engage with me.

I want to transform your understanding of your economic life, while at the same time help you bridge the gaps among your spiritual, psychological, mental, and social life in such a way that deepens your awareness of what you are capable of creating in this world.

In short, I want to talk to you and give you the place to talk to me.

The quickest way to do that is to sign in to the Michael E. Gerber Club (www.michaelegerberclub.com). Come visit me, and join a host of others whose entrepreneur is awakening within, whose passion it is to create a new and significantly more exciting life, and whose desire it is to transform the world they live in.

That's what we talk about in the Michael E. Gerber Club. That's my reason for creating it. For you, for me, for all those like us who are tired of sitting around and waiting for something miraculous to happen.

Guess what. It already is happening. Everywhere you look. There is nothing to wait for. There is nothing to hope for. It is all there, already, waiting inside of you, as well as outside of you.

The miracles are happening every day. I see them. I participate in them. I stand witness to them.

I stand witness to you.
A poem I wrote some years ago says it best:

When you woke up this morning, all was before you. The
sun, the moon, the stars, the planets, the earth, and all upon
the earth, and every stunning galaxy, and the galaxies within
every single galaxy, and every joyous living thing was before
you, waiting in its place as though ordered to be still, so that
you could emerge from your sleep to engage, to play your
part, to begin the dance, the holy promise, the whirling, the
song, the breath.
And that mystery has happened every day of your life.
And that mystery will happen every day of the rest of your
life, until that day when you no longer wake up to play.
But, even then, it will all go on.
It will all go on.
Breathe into it, Sleeper.
Breath into it, and awaken to play.

Come Dream With Me,

Michael E. Gerber
Chief Dreamer
Chief Dreamer Enterprises
Carlsbad, California
www.michaelegerber.com

Resources

In 2007, Michael Gerber founded Chief Dreamer Enterprises a holding company comprising a network of turnkey enterprises to awaken the entrepreneur within the world and provide the vast array of resources needed to flourish and grow awakened entreprenuers and their companies.

For resources that support the principles in this book, we invite you to go to www.michaelegerber.com and select the *reSources* page. This site will feature and regularly update all of the resources and tools that Chief Dreamer Enterprises launches to serve what Michael Gerber refers to as *The New Entrepreneur*. Check the site often as new products are developed or improved all the time!

At www.michaelegerber.com you will find resources that include the following.

THE MICHAEL E. GERBER CLUB

This is a perfect place to start your journey. The Michael E. Gerber Club is all about creating a venture, company, business, enterprise—whatever you choose to call it—that exemplifies the best you can be on behalf of all of those people who deeply need what you can do for them. The world needs what you have to offer!

Not sure what that is, just yet? Let's talk and let's figure it out together.

That's the purpose of the Michael E. Gerber Club: To move you from where you are to where you're meant to go. To move your spirit to a higher place than it's ever been before. To expand your horizons, to reach deep down in your soul, where life is hiding, where spirit awakens itself, where the entrepreneur within you explodes with creativity and action.

Imagine being able to interact, ask questions, make comments, get advice, and get direction directly from Michael E. Gerber! Interact with him and the group about your business, your life, what's working, what's not working, or just listen in and absorb all the great dialogue going on with its members. The cost of this extraordinary opportunity, to be mentored by the business coach that *Inc.* magazine calls "The World's #1 Small Business Guru!" is only $39.95 each month. Even if you can only participate in one call a month, The Michael E. Gerber Club is an extraordinary experience and an investment in your future.

Resource: www.michaelegerber.com.

THE DREAMING ROOM

Feeling stuck? Not sure what you should be, could be, want to be doing for the rest of your life? Not certain that the business you own is the right one for you, or is doing what you really want it to do? Is your business driving you crazy with "busy, busy, busy"? Has the tyranny of routine that so many of us get lost in, confused by, and debilitated with, captured you and your life?

Well, then, the Dreaming Room is exactly the experience you need.

In the Dreaming Room you will discover the unique process Michael Gerber has invented to awaken the entrepreneur within you, by discovering the four personalities of the awakened entrepreneur—the dreamer, the thinker, the storyteller, and the leader.

Discover how these four personalities begin the process of "beginner's mind, on a blank piece of paper."

And that's why the Dreaming Room is unlike any 2½–day experience you have ever had. If your business has lost its passion, if your life has lost its direction, if your imagination has come to a crossroads and you know not which road to take, you must attend this life-altering event.

The Dreaming Room will awaken a new fire and focus within you, alter your thinking, change the way you see yourself, and help you to create endless possibilities for your life and your business.

Resource: www.michaelegerber.com.

MICHAEL E. GERBER SPEAKING

Michael E. Gerber doesn't just speak; he electrifies audiences all around the world by inspiring them to dream. He awakens infinite options in his listeners for the pursuit of the impossible.

He drives home the extraordinary and eviscerates the ordinary, bringing everyone to that most special place in the world — that place where their imaginations begin to soar. That place Michael E. Gerber calls the Dreaming Room.

"Wake up!" Michael Gerber says. "Wake up and see what's missing in your life, in your business, in your work, in your job, in your relationships. And then, when you see what's missing, go to work *on* your business, go to work *on* your life, go to work *on* your job, to create what you've always wanted, but somehow lost."

"You can have everything you want in your life," Michael E. Gerber asserts. "All you need to do is to see it, explore it, invent it, and pursue it with earnest passion. And, I'll show you how."

Michael E. Gerber will ignite new energy into your audience, and they will be forever changed and grateful to you for the experience.

Resource: www.michaelegerber.com.

BEYOND PERSONAL GROWTH

Over the past 30 years, the personal growth industry has skyrocketed into a multi-billion-dollar business. Seminars, workshops, week-long intensives, overnights, yearlong master's programs—you name it; it's out there. Whatever someone can put between two covers to promise you a new life, they will publish and people will buy.

Why then, do so few lives truly work?

Why is it that with all the "new age" solutions, spiritual gurus, personal growth giants, and so many, many "experts" out there, does the world suffer in the same ways that it did before all of the hoopla began?

The answer is clear to anyone who is open to reflect upon the question: Personal growth doesn't happen in a seminar, in a coaching relationship, or in a Zen dojo. It happens somewhere else. We have the answer to the personal growth question that each and every one of you have asked, are asking, and will continue to ask: "How do I grow beyond where I am, to live a life I have never lived before?" We found it. We created it. Beyond Personal Growth™ is our answer. *The* answer!

It is a simple, no-nonsense formula, designed to awaken the true spirit of discovery within you. By setting out tasks, goals, and assignments in the practical world—the world in which you live—it will move you toward the transformational experience of internal growth.

Resource: www.michaelegerber.com/ven_beyond_personal _growth.php.

FOUND MONEY

Michael Gerber has been in the business of fixing broken businesses for more than 30 years. During that time his companies and he have fixed tens of thousands of them. He realized during these years that the one piece that he hadn't yet mastered was how to address the capital question.

Where do broken businesses find the capital they need, to not only fix themselves but to expand their capability to grow beyond their current limitations?

You might also have that problem. But more than likely, if you're like the tens of thousands of businesses he's fixed, you probably don't even know that you do. Certified Capital Advisors™ is the company he created to solve that problem. Rather than going *outside* your company to find the money you need, his partner Steve Wilkinghoff and he will teach you how to go *inside* your company to find the money you need.

Yes, believe it or not, we can find the missing money *inside* your current business. How can they find money in your business when *you* can't find it? Well, the answer to that question is simple: *They know where to look for it!*

Resource: Certified Capital Advisors at www.michaele gerber.com.

GROW YOUR BUSINESS

Entrepreneurs and small business owners must be focused. And their focus must be on one thing. And that one thing is growth.

To not grow your company is to deny it the life it was born to fulfill. A company that has the potential to serve millions, but is serving only hundreds, is being deprived of its true destiny.

Why don't most new businesses grow? It's because there are so few who understand the mechanics, the energy, and the mind-set needed to set a company on its natural path of growth, to sustain that process, and to stimulate its reach to higher levels of performance every company—yes, even yours!—is destined to fulfill.

My Growth Resources™ is an online turnkey services center in development to provide you with the exact resources you need to fulfill your destiny.

On our site, you will find My Growth Managers™, My Growth Partners™, My Growth Accountants™, My Growth Attorneys™, My Growth Capital™, My Growth Software™, and many, many more.

What's the difference between a growth manager and an ordinary manager? My growth managers are certified to possess the entrepreneurial support capability every growth business needs to go the extra mile.

Resource: www.michaelegerber.com.

THE MICHAEL E. GERBER COACH

Michael Gerber invented coaching in 1977, long before the words "business coaching" came into being. He invented it when he came to the inspired conclusion that most small business owners don't know how to build a flourishing business. And the reason they don't know is because the vast majority of them are not entrepreneurs. They are "technicians suffering from an entrepreneurial seizure."

The outcome of that epiphany is what he now calls the Michael E. Gerber Coach, the only business development model that truly works. Its success is demonstrated by its unique transformation of thousands of small businesses throughout the world thousands upon thousands of times.

Is your business ready to grow?

Is your business stuck in the miasma of not knowing what needs to be done?

Are you caught up in "doing it, doing it, doing it," without a clear path to liberate yourself from the work that keeps you enslaved with all the little things that should be done by others, but isn't? Instead, it's being done by you. Or, worse yet, it isn't being done at all. You can't grow a company that way.

Resource: www.michaelegerber.com.

ORGANIZE YOUR BUSINESS

Believe it. Every single one of the thousands of businesses we have walked into was hopelessly disorganized.

Look on your desk. Look in the drawers of your desk. Look in the closets of your home office. Look in the trunk or glove compartment or the front seat of your car. I can guess what you'll find—an unbelievable mess! Finding something on your desk is equivalent to an archeological dig.

But that's not all. What you see in front of you is only the visible mess that exists in most small businesses. That mess also exists deeper within the foundation of your business and in most people's lives!

Why is it that order escapes everybody's attention?

Why is it that most of the people you know haven't a clue on how to "get organized"?

Why is it that so few of us realize that order, cleanliness, consistency, and control are essential skills that every small business owner, every entrepreneur, and every company of any size must master?

The Michael E. Gerber Organizer™ is being created to do just that. Just for you. For the messy guy in your life. For the one who craves order, can't stand to live without order, but hasn't a clue what to do to achieve that order. We can help!

Resource: www.michaelegerber.com.

CAPITALIZE YOUR BUSINESS

Once you've found the money *inside* your company, it will eventually become necessary to find the money *outside* your company.

The truth is, very, very few of us have ever figured out how to do that. And even if we do, we most often sacrifice too much to get it—too much equity, too much control, too much of the spirit that moved us to create the company we've built.

Fear not! There's a much better way.

At the Entrepreneur Capital Corporation™, we call it the Cash Flow Solution™. With the Cash Flow Solution you will be able to attract investors to your company.

Not by giving them equity in return for the capital they invest, but by giving them an agreed upon share of your Cash Flow.

Just think! Not only will you maintain ownership of your company, but you will raise the needed Growth Capital, and pay for it through the revenue generated by that infusion of cash. Not a bad idea!

Resource: www.michaelegerber.com.